THIRD EDITION

TELECOURSE STUDY GUIDE TO

GOVERNMENT BY CONSENT
A NATIONAL PERSPECTIVE

SUE LEE

DALLAS COUNTY COMMUNITY COLLEGE DISTRICT

KENDALL/HUNT PUBLISHING COMPANY
2460 Kerper Boulevard P.O. Box 539 Dubuque, Iowa 52004-0539

Acknowledgements

Special thanks are extended to every one at the R. Jan LeCroy Center for Educational Telecommunications who participated in the production of *Government by Consent*, especially to John Forshee, Content Specialist; Nora Busby, Instructional Design; Margot A. Olson, Test Design; Lee Hoffman, Editor; Nancy Ward and the desktop publishing staff at The Word Works; and Karen D. Pate, Eastfield College Photographer.

For their assistance in the production of *Government by Consent*, we express our appreciation to Pamela K. Quinn, Director of the Center for Educational Telecommunications; Bob Crook, Executive Producer; the Marketing Staff; and to the Local Advisory Board: Lynn Brink, Kathyrn Yates, and Noreen Warwick. Special thanks to Deborah Wood for the photograph used with Lesson 13.

Sue Lee

This *Government by Consent* telecourse is produced by the Dallas County Community College District, Center for Educational Telecommunications in association with Coast Community College District, State of Florida Department of Education, Higher Education Telecommunications Association of Oklahoma, Michigan Community College Association, Northern Illinois Learning Resources Cooperative, and Tarrant County Junior College District.

Formerly entitled STUDENT'S GUIDE TO AMERICAN GOVERNMENT SURVEY, Fourth Edition

This edition has been printed directly from camera ready copy.

Printed in the United States of America
10 9 8 7 6 5 4 3 2 1

Table of Contents

To the Student

The purpose of *Govenment by Consent* is to give you a solid foundation for becoming an informed, knowledgeable, and active participant in the government of the United States. But that is just a beginning. Whenever you watch the evening news or pick up a daily newspaper, the spotlight will shine on some event reflecting what you learn in this exciting telecourse.

As our production team was completing its work, Supreme Court rulings on flag burning and abortion highlighted the Court's role as interpreter of the U.S. Constitution. The decisions also illustrated federal-state issues and the impact of the Bill of Rights on individual rights.

Ethics questions in the House of Representatives caused two last-minute changes. Thomas S. Foley was interviewed in the telelessons as majority whip of the House of Representatives and William Gray, when he was chair of the House Budget Committee. Before we went to press, Tom Foley had become speaker of the House and William Gray, majority whip.

As we wrap up this course, the U.S. Constitution has twenty-six amendments. But whether you study it next year or ten years from now, new amendments will be proposed continuously—and perhaps one or more will be ratified.

In 1963 Martin Luther King Jr. wrote a remarkable "Letter from Birmingham City Jail." It is reprinted at the back of this Study Guide partly because he sums up so many different aspects of this course and partly because it gives you a first-person account of how one person applied his knowledge of American government in a way that still affects millions of people today.

The excitement and change in this dynamic form of government is what first attracted me to a career in political science. I hope you, too, will be caught up in the vitality of Thomas Jefferson's "golden notion" as we move forward in its third century. The combination of television and textbook, directed by this Study Guide, should help you see not only how the U.S. government affects you, but—even more important—how you make it work!

Course Organization

Government by Consent is designed as a comprehensive learning system consisting of three elements: Study Guide, textbook, and telelessons.

Study Guide

This Study Guide acts as your daily instructor. For each lesson it gives you an overview, the learning objectives, textbook reading assignment, focus points, key terms for both textbook and telelesson, recommended readings, projects for becoming involved, and a self test. If you follow the Study Guide recommendations for reading and view each lesson carefully, you should successfully accomplish all of the requirements for this course.

Textbook

Schmidt, Steffen W., Mack C. Shelley II, and Barbara A. Bardes. *American Goverent and Politics Today,* 1993-94 edition. St. Paul, Minn.: West Publishing Company, 1993.

The textbook offers an interesting presentation of facts and sidelights about the U.S. system of government. Key terms are defined in side margins. The specific reading assignment for each lesson appears in the Study Guide, just ahead of the Textbook Focus Points. Be sure to read this material *before* viewing the telelesson.

Telelessons

Each telelesson is correlated with the textbook reading assignment for that lesson. The telelessons are packed with information, so watch them closely. If the lessons are broadcast more than once in your area, or if video or audio tapes are available at your college, you might find it helpful to watch the telelessons more than once or to listen to an audio tape for review. Since examination questions will be taken from the telelessons as well as from the textbook, careful attention to both is vital to your success.

Study Guidelines

This Study Guide acts as your daily instructor by organizing the material for you and pointing out important aspects of each lesson. Use the following guidelines for each lesson:

1. Read the **Overview, Learning Objectives, Key Terms** and **Textbook Focus Points** for the lesson.

2. Complete the **Textbook Reading Assignment**, keeping the **Key Terms** and **Textbook Focus Points** in mind.

3. Write out your responses to the **Textbook Focus Points**, going back to the text if you aren't certain you know the answers.

4. Read the names of the major **Telelesson Interviewees**, then look over the **Telelesson Focus Points**.

5. View the telelesson with the **Key Terms** and **Telelesson Focus Points** in mind. Take only brief notes while viewing.

6. Write out detailed responses to the **Telelesson Focus Points** immediately after you have seen it, referring to your notes to help you.

7. Now go back and define each **Key Term**.

8. Take the **Self Test** to check your understanding of the concepts presented in the lesson.

9. Compare your answers to the **Answer Key** located at the end of the lesson. If you answered incorrectly, the key provides references so that you can review the material from which each question was taken.

10. Extend your learning by studying some of the **Recommended Readings** and acting on one or more of the suggestions for **Getting Involved**.

Government and You

Overview

The title of this lesson, "Government and You," actually describes both this lesson and all of those that follow. The title of this course, *Government by Consent*, indicates who gives the government of the United States of America its power to make rules and see that they are followed: we, the people.

Those of us who were born in other countries, and choose to become U.S. citizens, promise to support this country's government during our naturalization ceremony. But those of us born here don't sign a contract saying that we agree to be governed by the rules of the United States of America. Instead, we give our consent tacitly, by not working to overthrow the government or to drastically change its basic organization and principles.

Yet all of us also show our consent to be governed in this fashion when we actively support the individuals and the issues we believe are best or right for our country—just as much as when we use our power to change the persons we elect to represent us, or the rules they make, when we believe they are bad or wrong for our country. By thus giving our consent to be so governed, we allow the government of the United States to make decisions that control, direct, and influence each one of our lives.

In this lesson, and indeed throughout this course, we examine what the U.S. government does. We see how it affects almost every aspect of our lives—literally from the moment of conception or immigration here until well after we die.

But who comprises this government, and whom we let decide what it is going to do, also is our responsibility—a responsibility which we can accept or relinquish. For as citizens of these United States it is we ourselves who "consent to be so governed."

This lesson defines terms we frequently use, such as "government," "politics," "power," "democracy," and "liberty." Even more important, it shows how these words apply to us.

Life is a series of choices: We either make these choices ourselves or let someone else make them for us. The same is true for the American form of government: We can become personally involved and participate, or we can choose not to become involved, not participate, and let others act in our place. Either way, we live with the consequences of our decision.

The problem of how to help, or what to do about, homeless people is only one of many issues facing this nation today. But it illustrates—both for them and for every one of us—how we choose what the relationship will be between our government and its people. The television portion of this lesson identifies who some of these people are, investigates how they arrived in this situation, outlines possible solutions to the problem and, overall, addresses the ultimate question of how this might best be accomplished.

In every aspect of our lives, we have surprising power to influence the conduct of our government, to affect the choices that government makes in our behalf. Today, more than ever, it is up to us to learn how to use that power to make the best choices for ourselves and our nation—and, in the process, for generations to come.

Learning Objectives

Goal: The purpose of "Government and You" is to define the fundamental concepts forming the philosophical base of the government of the United States.

Objectives:

1. Define the fundamental concepts or forms of government, in terms of what it is and what it does.

2. Define the fundamental concept of American politics, with specific reference to resolving conflicts.

3. Explain the difference between "power" and "compliance," as they are exercised through citizen involvement in decision-making.

4. Describe the concept of democracy, specifically differentiating between direct and representative democracies as a basis for the common political heritage expressed by Thomas Jefferson's "golden notion."

5. Compare the two theories, elitism and pluralism, which illustrate approaches to formulating policies in our government.

6. Contrast the two most commonly held viewpoints, liberalism and conservatism, as they illustrate the basic American values of liberty, equality, and property.

7. List some of the trade-offs and compromises that government has to resolve when making choices for American society, and explain how individuals can affect these choices.

8. List the various levels of the hierarchy of political involvement, including who are likely and not likely to participate at each level.

9. Describe the homeless and their plight, as the government debates how to assist them.

Study Guidelines

Remember to follow the Study Guidelines presented on page vi.

Key Terms

Watch for these terms and pay particular attention to what each one means, as you follow the textbook and telelesson.

Institutions	Limited government
Politics	Universal suffrage
Authority	Elite theory
Government	Pluralism
Public policies	Political culture
Compliance	Political socialization
Legitimacy	Liberty
Power	Equality
Totalitarian	Inalienable rights
Anarchy	Popular sovereignty
Direct democracy	Ideology
Consent of the people	Liberalism
Representative democracy	Conservatism

Textbook Reading Assignment

Schmidt, Steffan W., Mark C. Shelley II, and Barbara A. Bardes. *American Government and Politics Today*, 1993-94 edition. St. Paul, Minn.: West Publishing Co., 1993. Chapter 1, "American Democracy and Political Culture," pp. 3-25.

Textbook Focus Points

Before you read the textbook assignment, review the following points to help focus your thoughts. After you complete the assignment, write out your responses to reinforce what you have learned.

1. What is the fundamental concept of American government, and how are we affected by this concept?

2. What are the major definitions of "politics," and how does politics resolve conflicts?

3. What is "government," and what does it do?

4. What is "compliance," and why do people comply with government decisions?

5. What is "power," and how can it be exercised?

6. What is a "democracy," and what is the ideal form of a democracy?

7. Why did the founders fear a "direct democracy"?

8. What is a "representative democracy," and how is it practiced in the United States?

---

9. What two theories describe who makes policy decisions in the United States?

10. What gives Americans a common political heritage?

11. What are the two most commonly held ideologies within the American electorate?

Telelesson Interviewees

The following individuals share their expertise in the telelesson:

Richard Knight–Former City Manager, Dallas, Texas
William S. Sinclair–City Manager, St. Joseph, Michigan
F.G. Sweet–Member of the Clergy; Director, Crossroads Mission, Dallas, Texas
Jay Van Den Berg–Co-Vice Chair, Community Economic Development Corporation, St. Joseph, Michigan

Telelesson Focus Points

Before viewing the telelesson, read over the following points to help focus your thoughts. After the presentation, write out your responses to help you remember these important points.

1. What was Thomas Jefferson's "golden notion," penned in the Declaration of Independence, and how else can it be expressed?

2. How can individuals shape the institutions that make binding decisions for society, and how many people actually become involved?

3. What are some of the theories developed to determine why people don't participate in government?

4. What does government do for us?

5. What are some of the trade-offs and compromises that government has to resolve when making choices for American society?

6. What are the issues regarding government assistance to the homeless?

7. What are the various levels of the hierarchy of political involvement, and who is likely to participate at each level?

Recommended Reading

The following suggestions are not required unless your instructor assigns them. They are listed to let you know where you can find additional information on areas which interest you.

Doan, Michael. "What a Life Is Worth: U.S. Seeks a Price." *U.S. News & World Report* 99 (September 15, 1985): p. 58.

Gray, Paul. "Another Look at Democracy in America." *Time* 127 (June 16, 1986): pp. 99-100.

"How Our Government Works." *U.S. News & World Report* 98 (January 28, 1985): pp. 37-54.

Lasswell, Harold. *Politics: Who Gets What, When, and How.* New York: McGraw-Hill, 1936.

Toffler, Alvin. *The Third Wave.* New York: Random House, 1982.

Getting Involved

These activities are not required unless your instructor assigns them. But they offer good suggestions to help you understand and become more involved in the political process.

1. Note the "Getting Involved" section in your textbook at the end of Chapter 1.

2. Write to the World Future Society [4916 St. Elmo Avenue; Bethesda, Maryland 20814-5089] to learn if there is a local chapter in your community. Ask the organization to send you information about what is being done by citizens in your community to impact governmental decision-making about the future.

Self Test

After reading the assignment and watching the telelesson, you should be able to answer these questions. When you have completed the test, turn to the Answer Key to score your answers.

1. The most fundamental concept of U.S. government is that the
   a. United States is a direct democracy.
   b. United States is the "melting pot" of the world.
   c. people control the government.
   d. people have inalienable rights.

2. Most major definitions of politics are based on the concept of
   a. abundant resources.
   b. real political problems.
   c. social conflict.
   d. some type of limited democracy.

3. For most societies, government is
   a. based on a form of democracy.
   b. not relevant to the average person in his or her daily activity.
   c. ultimately the authority which allocates values.
   d. formulated by individuals who have received formal training.

4. A major reason that the public will comply with the decisions of the U.S. government is that the people
   a. understand that government makes nearly all the decisions.
   b. consider government to be sacred.
   c. believe government actions are appropriate, legal and correct.
   d. will do as they are told.

5. Perhaps a more fundamental answer as to why we comply with rules we don't like is because we understand that the government
   a. can be changed with any election.
   b. decides what is best for us.
   c. will make fair laws to govern us.
   d. has the power to enforce the laws.

6. A system of government in which the ultimate political authority is vested in the people is called
   a. an anarchy.
   b. a democracy.
   c. a dictatorship.
   d. the proletariat.

7. For many centuries, any form of democracy was considered
   a. a dangerous and unstable approach to government.
   b. the only legitimate form of government.
   c. a major obstacle to communism.
   d. the best form of government that could be devised.

8. The framers of the Constitution settled on a republican form of government in which people elect some of their own to make laws and policy, also called a
   a. direct democracy.
   b. representative democracy.
   c. legitimate democracy.
   d. bureaucratic democracy.

9. Because American society is so large and complex, ordinary citizens cannot really make policy decisions with their votes; instead, these decisions are made by
   a. the masses or the aristocracy.
   b. the oligarchy or the monarchy.
   c. elites or pluralists.
   d. labor or business.

10. Americans have a common political culture because
   a. the government sets forth specific guidelines of acceptable social actions.
   b. the country has more than one political party.
   c. the country has a heterogeneous population.
   d. Americans have a patterned way of thinking about the government.

11. The two relatively moderate positions on the American political spectrum that have dominated for decades are
   a. liberalism and conservatism.
   b. elitism and pluralism.
   c. majority and minority.
   d. socialism and capitalism.

12. In the Declaration of Independence, Thomas Jefferson wrote that individuals should establish "a government deriving its just powers from the consent of the governed," meaning that the government
    a. has the power to govern the people.
    b. obtains authority from the people.
    c. makes laws that people must obey.
    d. allows people to have a voice.

13. Which of the following methods of participation is **NOT** used by people to shape the institutions that make binding decisions for society?
    a. Their contributions
    b. Their votes
    c. Their fulfillment of military obligations
    d. Their participation in the political process

14. One theory about why more people don't participate in government centers on the notion that
    a. people are not aware of the need for them to participate.
    b. the majority of people are too egocentric.
    c. governmental structure doesn't allow access into the system.
    d. people are overwhelmed by government's complexity.

15. The major business of government at all levels is
    a. making choices about which issues to address.
    b. protecting its citizens from invasion.
    c. regulating intrastate commerce.
    d. exploring new frontiers.

16. Since there are limits to the resources that government has at its disposal, government must
    a. cultivate international agreements.
    b. prioritize society's needs.
    c. analyze the total cost of each project.
    d. tax each citizen.

17. Which of the following is NOT an issue regarding government assistance to the homeless?
    a. Are the homeless a responsibility of the government?
    b. What are the trade-offs in dealing with the homeless?
    c. Is the homeless problem serious enough for government to become involved?
    d. What are the costs for government to solve the homeless problem?

18. Those who exercise their power to influence the choices that government makes on our behalf form
    a. the social-conflict pyramid.
    b. Maslow's hierarchy of needs.
    c. the wheel of representative democracy.
    d. the hierarchy of political involvement.

Short-Answer Question:
19. Describe how government pervades and influences our lives each day.

Answer Key

These are the correct answers with reference to the Learning Objectives, and to the source of the information: the Textbook Focus Points, Schmidt, *et al. American Government and Politics Today* (Schmidt), and the Telelesson Focus Points. Page numbers are also given for the Textbook Focus Points. "KT" indicates questions with Key Terms defined.

Question	Answer	Learning Objective	Textbook Focus Point (page no.)	Telelesson Focus Point
1	C	1	1 (Schmidt, p. 5)	
2	C	2	2 (Schmidt, p. 6)............KT	
3	C	1	3 (Schmidt, p. 7)............KT	
4	C	3	4 (Schmidt, p. 8)	
5	D	3	5 (Schmidt, p. 8)	
6	B	4	6 (Schmidt, p. 9)	
7	A	4	7 (Schmidt, p. 10)	
8	B	4	8 (Schmidt, p. 12)............KT	
9	C	5	9 (Schmidt, pp.13-15)	
10	D	4	10 (Schmidt, p. 15)............KT	
11	A	6	11 (Schmidt, p. 20)............KT	
12	B	4		1
13	C	7		2
14	D	8		3
15	A	1		4
16	B	7		5
17	C	9		6
18	D	8		7

Short Answer:

19		1,7		4,5

The Living Constitution

Overview

The Constitution of the United States of America did not spring up fully formed out of nowhere, when the colonies declared their independence from Great Britain in 1776. Instead, it evolved in a slow, and often painful, process of trial and error over more than 150 years.

In 1620, the pilgrims provided one of the earliest documents establishing a democratic form of government. The Mayflower Compact served as a prototype for the Constitution, because it contained the essential ingredient: It depended on the consent of the people involved.

However, the first formal attempt at creating a national government in this country produced agreement on the Articles of Confederation. Once the Articles were put into practice, it didn't take long for the founders to discover that, while this document did form a "United States," it also had serious deficiencies. The Philadelphia Convention, later called the Constitutional Convention, was called for May 1787 to address these deficiencies.

Much has been written and debated about the Constitutional Convention: the men, motives, compromises, and results. The story continues to fascinate us today. But the truly remarkable point about the document that this convention produced, the Constitution of the United States of America, is that it has remained intact with relatively few formal changes for over two hundred years. Why this is true is the focus of this lesson.

As we look at "The Living Constitution," we examine the process these founders used to develop the U.S. structure of government, as well as the document they wrote to provide the framework for governing this nation. The Constitution has been criticized for its vagueness, but the framers deliberately provided an outline of the basic structure of government, leaving the details to be filled in by future generations.

We also concentrate on some of the formal and informal changes that have taken place since the Constitution was written, allowing this document to keep pace with technological advancements, population growth, and shifts in societal mores. The Constitution written over two hundred years ago "lives" today through custom and usage, judicial interpretation, and the amendment process.

Learning Objectives

Goal: The purpose of "The Living Constitution" is to develop awareness of the U.S. Constitution as a "living" document, capable of being adapted to technological advancements, population growth, and shifts in societal mores.

Objectives:

1. Describe the political events and relevant documents—such as the Mayflower Compact, Articles of Confederation, and Declaration of Independence—which provided the foundation upon which the U.S. Constitution was built.

2. Recognize the impact of the people who met at the Constitutional Convention—the delegates, their backgrounds, their recommended plans, and their compromises—on the final document which became the U.S. Constitution.

3. Evaluate the Constitution in terms of being a "living" document: its deliberate vagueness, the features of separation of power and checks and balances, and the addition of the Bill of Rights.

4. Explain the formal process of proposing and ratifying an amendment to the Constitution, noting how the ratification of Amendment Twenty-one differs from that of the others.

5. Use the examples of *Marbury v. Madison*, *Griswold v. Connecticut* and the establishment of political parties to explain the processes for changing the Constitution informally, through judicial review, judicial interpretation, and custom and usage.

6. Describe how individuals are involved today in changing the Constitution, using the examples of a proposed constitutional convention and the Equal Rights Amendment.

7. Justify measures that you as an individual might take to support constitutional change or maintain the status quo on a particular issue.

Study Guidelines

Remember to follow the Study Guidelines presented on page vi.

Key Terms

Watch for these terms and pay particular attention to what each one means, as you follow the textbook and telelesson.

Natural rights	Ratification
Consent of the governed	Federalists
Confederation	Anti-Federalists
Bicameral legislature	Judicial review
Supremacy doctrine	Eighteenth Amendment [Prohibition](TV)
Great Compromise	Twenty-first Amendment
Separation of powers	Griswold v. Connecticut (TV)
Checks and balances	*Equal Rights Amendment* (TV)
Electoral college	

Textbook Reading Assignment

Schmidt, Shelley, and Bardes. *American Government and Politics Today*, 1993-94 edition. Chapter 2, "The Constitution," pp. 27-62.

Textbook Focus Points

Before you read the textbook assignment, review the following points to help focus your thoughts. After you complete the assignment, write out your responses to reinforce what you have learned.

1. Why is the Mayflower Compact significant historically and politically?

2. What did the First Continental Congress accomplish, and how was this accepted by the British?

3. Why was the Declaration of Independence important, and what did it set forth?

4. What was accomplished under the Articles of Confederation?

5. What were the weaknesses of the Articles of Confederation?

6. Who were the men who actually wrote the Constitution, and what political experience did they have?

7. Explain the basic provisions of the Virginia Plan, the New Jersey Plan, and the Great Compromise, presented at the 1787 Constitutional Convention.

8. What were the major features of the new U.S. Constitution?

9. Why was the Bill of Rights needed, and from what documents was it drafted?

10. What is the formal method of amending the Constitution?

11. What are some of the informal methods for bringing about constitutional change?

Telelesson Interviewees

The following individuals share their expertise in the telelesson:

Jesse Choper–Dean and Professor, University of California Law School, Berkeley
Archibald Cox–Professor, Harvard University Law School
Eleanor Holmes-Norton–Professor, Georgetown University Law School

Telelesson Focus Points

Before viewing the telelesson, read over the following points to help focus your thoughts. After the presentation, write out your responses to help you remember these important points.

1. Why is the U.S. Constitution called a "living" document?

2. What is one major constitutional change brought about through custom and usage?

3. How does the Twenty-first Amendment differ from the other twenty-five?

4. Of what significance is *Griswold v. Connecticut* in the process of judicial review bringing about constitutional change?

5. Why do some people fear a constitutional convention today?

6. How can individuals be involved in the process of constitutional change, such as with the Equal Rights Amendment?

Recommended Reading

The following suggestions are not required unless your instructor assigns them. They are listed to let you know where you can find additional information on areas which interest you.

Beard, Charles A. *An Economic Interpretation of the Constitution*. New York: Macmillan, 1913.

Boles, Janet. *The Politics of the Equal Rights Amendment*. New York: Longman's, 1979.

Storing, Herbert J. *What the Anti-Federalists Were For*. Chicago: University of Chicago Press, 1981.

Warren, Charles. *The Making of the Constitution*. New York: Barnes & Noble, 1967.

Getting Involved

These activities are not required unless your instructor assigns them. But they offer good suggestions to help you understand and become more involved in the political process.

1. Select one of the leaders of the Constitutional Convention, and write a paper about how that person contributed to the new Constitution.

2. Note the "Getting Involved" section in your textbook at the end of Chapter 2.

3. Search out and read the constitution of another country. Compare it with the U.S. Constitution. Then write a brief paper on what you believe are the strengths and weaknesses of each constitution.

Self Test

After reading the assignment and watching the telelesson, you should be able to answer these questions. When you have completed the test, turn to the Answer Key to score your answers.

1. The historical and political significance of the *Mayflower Compact* was that it
   a. established an American settlement under a royal charter.
   b. started the first settlement in America.
   c. depended on the consent of the individuals involved.
   d. established peaceful relations with the natives.

2. The first Continental Congress was called by the colonies for the purpose of
   a. revolting against Great Britain.
   b. expressing colonial grievances to the King.
   c. planning for a peaceful independence from Great Britain.
   d. coordinating education and religion.

3. Perhaps the most revolutionary concept in the Declaration of Independence was the assumption that
   a. people have natural rights.
   b. government must be obeyed even when it is wrong.
   c. each person is more important than the whole of society.
   d. females are the equal of males.

4. Accomplishments under the Articles of Confederation included the
   a. settlement of certain states' claims to western lands.
   b. right of the central government to demand revenues from the states.
   c. ability to make easy changes when needed.
   d. authority to force states to take action in a time of crisis.

5. The most serious weakness of the national government established under the Articles of Confederation was the relationship between the
   a. states and the central government.
   b. thirteen sovereign states.
   c. United States and Great Britain.
   d. United States and the Indian tribes.

6. Although Congress had the legal right to declare war and to conduct foreign policy under the Articles of Confederation, it did not have the right to
   a. commission officers from the state militias.
   b. demand revenues from the states.
   c. train the states' militias.
   d. build battleships for a navy.

7. Delegates to the 1787 Constitutional Convention were representative of
   a. the general population.
   b. elder statesmen.
   c. military power.
   d. the economically elite.

8. The Virginia Plan presented at the 1787 Constitutional Convention worked to the advantage of
   a. small states.
   b. large states.
   c. large and small states.
   d. none of the states.

9. The New Jersey Plan presented at the 1787 Constitutional Convention was
   a. simply an amendment to the Articles of Confederation.
   b. an attempt to create a new and powerful central government.
   c. advocated by large, populous states.
   d. designed to have a single person in charge of the executive branch.

10. The Great Compromise of the 1787 Constitutional Convention proposed a
    a. unicameral legislature in which each state would have one vote.
    b. slave-free nation in all but the southern states.
    c. bicameral legislature.
    d. plural executive branch.

11. The concept of separation of powers was included in the U.S. Constitution to prevent a major dispute over power between
    a. federal and state governments.
    b. state governments.
    c. House and Senate.
    d. any individuals or bodies.

12. One of the fundamental principles of the U.S. Constitution is control by the people, also known as
    a. popular sovereignty.
    b. judicial review.
    c. natural rights.
    d. a social contract.

13. A mandatory imperative was written into the Bill of Rights to command
    a. maximum flexibility for Congress when considering individual rights.
    b. protection for the power of state governments.
    c. increased power for Congress and the central government.
    d. safeguards for the rights of individuals.

14. The formal process for amending the U.S. Constitution allows
    a. an easy two-step procedure that has resulted in numerous changes.
    b. a difficult procedure that has resulted in few amendments.
    c. Congress to alter the Constitution without approval by the states.
    d. the president to veto any proposed amendments.

15. A national convention for the purpose of changing the Constitution can be proposed by
    a. a majority of the public.
    b. the Senate.
    c. the president.
    d. two-thirds of the states.

16. Informal methods of constitutional change include
    a. Congress passing legislation with a three-fourths majority.
    b. state governments changing their constitutions to supersede the U.S. Constitution.
    c. changing interpretations over time.
    d. twenty state governments agreeing on a specific change.

17. The Constitution is called a "living" document because
    a. legends of the founders live on.
    b. the problems of 1787 are the same as those we face today.
    c. judicial review is still in use today.
    d. amendments and interpretations allow it to meet changing needs.

18. Nowhere in the almost seven thousand words of the Constitution is there a provision for
    a. the president to inform the Congress.
    b. special-jurisdiction state courts.
    c. constitutional change.
    d. a system of political parties.

19. The only amendment to the U.S. Constitution that was ratified by state ratifying conventions rather than by state legislatures is the
    a. Eleventh Amendment.
    b. Nineteenth Amendment.
    c. Twenty-first Amendment.
    d. Twenty-sixth Amendment.

20. *Griswold v. Connecticut* helped establish a precedent for other privacy cases, by using the principle of judicial review to declare that
    a. a law prohibiting the use of contraceptives is unconstitutional.
    b. Connecticut law should be strictly enforced.
    c. the U.S. Supreme Court should let the state of Connecticut make laws regarding family planning.
    d. the right to privacy cannot be found in the Constitution.

21. Some people fear that a national constitutional convention called by Congress will
    a. set a precedent that may make it difficult to pass legislation in the future.
    b. reduce the president's initiative in establishing domestic policy.
    c. create additional issues which the Supreme Court must decide.
    d. act on a wide range of issues rather than just solving the particular issue for which it is called.

22. You may have a direct impact on constitutional change by
    a. reading the U.S. Constitution and advocating the overthrow of the government.
    b. helping to elect candidates who support the issues you favor and participating in protest marches.
    c. leading discussions at church and teaching a class on the biblical principles in the Constitution.
    d. deciding to run for Congress and introducing legislation to establish a unitary government.

23. The proposed Equal Rights Amendment was controversial in that it was the only amendment to be
    a. fraudulent in the purpose for which it was introduced.
    b. written to repeal a previous amendment.
    c. ratified by some states that later reversed their decisions.
    d. approved by state conventions rather than by state legislatures.

Short-Answer Questions:
24.   Describe the concept of separation of powers, and explain why the writers included this concept within the framework of the Constitution.

25.   Describe what measures you would take to support constitutional change or to maintain the status quo on a specific issue.

Answer Key

These are the correct answers with reference to the Learning Objectives, and to the source of the information: the Textbook Focus Points, Schmidt, *et al. American Government and Politics Today* (Schmidt), and the Telelesson Focus Points. Page numbers are also given for the Textbook Focus Points. "KT" indicates questions with Key Terms defined.

Question	Answer	Learning Objective	Textbook Focus Point (page no.)	Telelesson Focus Point
1	C	1	1 (Schmidt, p. 31)	
2	B	1	2 (Schmidt, p. 32)	
3	A	1	3 (Schmidt, p. 34)	KT
4	A	1	4 (Schmidt, p. 36)	
5	A	1	5 (Schmidt, p. 37)	
6	B	1	5 (Schmidt, p. 37)	
7	D	2	6 (Schmidt, p. 39)	
8	B	2	7 (Schmidt, p. 42)	
9	A	2	7 (Schmidt, p. 43)	
10	C	2	7 (Schmidt, p. 43)	KT
11	D	3	8 (Schmidt, p. 44)	KT
12	A	3	8 (Schmidt, p. 46)	
13	D	3	9 (Schmidt, p. 52)	
14	B	4	10 (Schmidt, p. 52)	
15	D	4	10 (Schmidt, p. 52)	
16	C	5	11 (Schmidt, p. 56)	
17	D	3		1
18	D	5		2
19	C	4	10 (Schmidt, p. 52)	KT....3
20	A	5		KT....4
21	D	6		5
22	B	6		6
23	C	6		KT....6

Short Answers:

24		2	8 (Schmidt, pp. 44-45)	
25		6,7		6

The Constitution in Crisis

Overview

Most of us do not even think about the Constitution of the United States until a crisis situation arises. But, like a road map on a dark night, the Constitution guides the government and its people in acting during a crisis. It serves as a source of stability and strength, when otherwise chaos would reign.

This lesson addresses five situations involving American presidents that created constitutional crises for our country: Andrew Jackson's defiance of a Supreme Court order regarding the Cherokee Indians, Abraham Lincoln confronted with the Civil War, Dwight D. Eisenhower facing the defiance of a court order by Arkansas Governor Orval Faubus, John F. Kennedy's assassination followed by Lyndon Johnson's succession to the presidency and the resulting vacancy in the vice-presidency, and the events leading to Richard Nixon's resignation. During these crises, the United States truly depended on the Constitution to guide the nation through each situation and to provide solutions to its problems.

The results of these crises show that the Constitution works. When the constitutional order of American government is challenged, the 200-year-old document proves to be a stabilizing force because of society's belief in it. Its adaptability keeps it alive and relevant. And its authority as the cornerstone of American government remains as strong as when it was first ratified.

Americans are committed to the ideal that everyone, with no exceptions, is subject to the rule of law.

Learning Objectives

Goal: The purpose of "The Constitution in Crisis" is to demonstrate the stabilizing force of the U.S. Constitution when crises in government occur.

Objectives:

1. Explain why the U.S. Constitution is effective during a crisis.

2. Outline the stabilizing effect of the Constitution when President Andrew Jackson defied the Supreme Court order in *Worcester v. Georgia*, regarding the Cherokee Indians.

3. Describe the dynamics of the U.S. Constitution as President Lincoln made executive decisions regarding the Civil War.

4. Explain how the Constitution influenced President Eisenhower as he dealt with Arkansas Governor Faubus's defiance of a federal court order.

5. Describe the constitutional crisis that arose when President Kennedy was assassinated and the significance of the Twenty-fifth Amendment for reacting to a constitutional crisis.

6. List those provisions of the Constitution that guided all three branches of the government during the Watergate Affair and the subsequent resignation of President Nixon.

Study Guidelines

Remember to follow the Study Guidelines presented on page vi.

Key Terms

Watch for these terms and pay particular attention to what each one means, as you follow the textbook and telelesson.

Executive privilege	Line of succession (TV)
Impeachment	Nationalize (TV)
Worcester v. Georgia (TV)	Twenty-fifth Amendment (TV)
Texas v. White (TV)	Watergate (TV)

Textbook Reading Assignment

Schmidt, Shelley, and Bardes. *American Government and Politics Today*, 1993-94 edition. Review Chapter 2, "The Constitution," pp. 27-62, then read the Twenty-Fifth Amendment in the appendix and the brief section on presidential impeachment in Chapter 13.

Textbook Focus Points

Because most of the information for this lesson is covered primarily in the telelesson, follow the Telelesson Focus Points.

Telelesson Interviewees

The following individuals share their expertise in the telelesson:

Archibald Cox–Professor, Harvard University Law School
Thomas Cronin–Professor of Political Science, The Colorado College
Randall Kennedy–Professor, Harvard University Law School

Telelesson Focus Points

Before viewing the telelesson, read over the following points to help focus your thoughts. After the presentation, write out your responses to help you remember these important points.

1. Why is the Constitution effective during a crisis?

2. What is the significance of *Worcester v. Georgia*?

3. What crisis did the Civil War pose for the Constitution?

4. What constitutional crisis occurred when Arkansas Governor Faubus refused to obey orders of the federal courts?

5. What crisis did President Kennedy's assassination create?

6. What is the significance of the Twenty-fifth Amendment in terms of solving a constitutional crisis?

7. What constitutional crisis did President Nixon create?

Recommended Reading

The following suggestions are not required unless your instructor assigns them. They are listed to let you know where you can find additional information on areas which interest you.

Bernstein, Carl, and Bob Woodward. *All the President's Men*. New York: Simon and Schuster, 1974.

Hazlitt, Henry. "The Vice Presidency." *Newsweek* (December 2, 1963): p. 48.

McKay, Robert. "Little Rock: Power Showdown." *The Nation* 185 (September 28, 1957): pp. 188-191.

"The Presidency." *Time* 82, no. 22 (November 29, 1963): pp. 21-32.

"What the 'Watergate Case' Is All About." *U.S. News & World Report* (September 25, 1972): pp. 27-29.

Getting Involved

These activities are not required unless your instructor assigns them. But they offer good suggestions to help you understand and become more involved in the political process.

1. Examine your state constitution and compare it with the U.S. Constitution. Note differences in structure, powers, individual rights, and flexibility provided in the two documents. Write a brief paper on how the differences between the two constitutions could create a crisis.

2. Select a period when the United States was without a vice president, before the Twenty-fifth Amendment was ratified in 1967. Write a brief essay about how the situation you chose might have changed if the Twenty-fifth Amendment had been in place at that time.

Self Test

After reading the assignment and watching the telelesson, you should be able to answer these questions. When you have completed the test, turn to the Answer Key to score your answers.

1. In a time of crisis, the Constitution is effective because it is
   a. very detailed and specific about the powers of each branch of government.
   b. specific about punishment for most offenses.
   c. adhered to and enforced by the people.
   d. not understood by most people.

2. In *Worcester v. Georgia*, a crisis arose when
   a. state laws applied to the Cherokee nation, and therefore Georgia had no jurisdiction over the Indians or their lands.
   b. the president of the United States refused to enforce the decision of the Supreme Court, and the Supreme Court could not force the president to carry out the decision.
   c. the State of Georgia was required to protect the Indians and their lands, but the governor refused to do so.
   d. the United States had made treaties with the Indians and given them lands that belonged to Georgia and Spain.

3. The constitutional crisis that climaxed in the Civil War concerned whether the
   a. Emancipation Proclamation was legally binding.
   b. union of the United States could be dissolved.
   c. troops that fired on Fort Sumter would be punished.
   d. Gettysburg Address would end the Civil War.

4. The issue in Little Rock, Arkansas, that created a constitutional crisis occurred when Governor Faubus refused to
   a. keep Arkansas within the Union.
   b. activate the Arkansas National Guard.
   c. obey orders of the federal courts.
   d. defend the state of Arkansas.

5. When President Eisenhower addressed the constitutional crisis in Little Rock, Arkansas, by nationalizing the Arkansas National Guard, he
   a. sent the state militia to train with the nation's troops in Germany.
   b. reviewed Arkansas troops during an inspection tour of Arkansas military bases.
   c. asked Arkansas to send volunteers to serve in the nation's forces for one year.
   d. placed the Arkansas guardsmen under his authority in order to carry out an order of the Supreme Court.

6. In 1963, the assassination of President John Kennedy created a constitutional crisis, because
   a. Lyndon Johnson had to resign as vice president before taking the oath of office as president.
   b. the Constitution did not provide a method of filling the office of vice president.
   c. there was great conflict between John Kennedy's cabinet and the people whom Lyndon Johnson wanted to appoint.
   d. Lyndon Johnson did not enjoy the great support for his programs that John Kennedy had for his.

7. The Twenty-fifth Amendment prevented another crisis by allowing the president to nominate a person to fill the post of vice president upon confirmation by a
   a. two-thirds vote of the Senate.
   b. three-fourths vote of the House of Representatives.
   c. majority vote of both houses of Congress.
   d. unanimous vote of the Supreme Court.

8. The possible impeachment of President Nixon and the decision of the Supreme Court in *U.S. v. Nixon* illustrates the basic constitutional principle
   a. of succession and disability.
   b. of executive privilege.
   c. that each person is entitled to a trial by jury.
   d. that no person is above the law.

9. During the constitutional crisis associated with President Nixon, the Supreme Court ruled on the doctrine of executive privilege, which is the right of the president to
   a. travel free of charge while in route to foreign policy conferences.
   b. preside over Congress when one house has adjourned.
   c. withhold information from or refuse to appear before a legislative committee.
   d. set the White House schedule when members of the presidential cabinet cannot agree.

10. Because of the constitutional crisis involving President Nixon, Congress followed provisions of the Constitution for impeachment and conviction, which
    a. cannot be used against an incumbent president.
    b. can only be applied to a president who has committed bribery or treason.
    c. will always result in the removal of a president from office.
    d. begin in the House of Representatives with articles of impeachment.

Short-Answer Question:
11. Do you believe that America is a nation of people or of laws? Why?

Answer Key

These are the correct answers with reference to the Learning Objectives and to the Telelesson Focus Points. "KT" indicates questions with Key Terms defined.

Question	Answer	Learning Objective	Telelesson Focus Point
1	C	1	1
2	B	2	KT...2
3	B	3	3
4	C	4	4
5	D	4	4
6	B	5	5
7	C	5	KT...6
8	D	6	
9	C	6	KT...7
10	D	6	KT...7

Short Answer:

11		1	1

Lesson 4

Federalism

Overview

When we hear the term "federalism," we usually think of the national government. However, federalism actually describes an overall form of government in which a written document, in our case the Constitution, spells out a division of power between the central national government and regional (state) governments.

Until we understand that concept, most of us are unaware that federalism affects us everyday. We may drive to work or on vacations over interstate highways; we can vote without having to scrimp to pay a poll tax or fearing intimidation; and we place our trash on the streets with little concern for how and where it will be disposed. These are examples of how power is divided among various levels of government. They also show how cooperation among these governments solves problems and serves the people on a daily basis, as well as during times of crisis.

This lesson defines federalism, explains why the founders adopted a federal system, describes the division of powers, and presents examples of common problems and of possible solutions to these problems. Keep in mind throughout the lesson that federalism is not a system of government far removed from us; instead, it provides a level of government best suited to address each problem and many points of public access.

Today, as our problems seem to grow larger and more complex each year, governments must work together to find solutions rather than becoming part of the problem themselves. Federalism is a grand experiment that will be successful as long as we participate in, work for, and demand responsive and effective government.

Learning Objectives

Goal: The purpose of "Federalism" is to illustrate why and how power is distributed between the national and state governments, and to explain how this distribution of power affords greater opportunity for individuals to participate in government.

Objectives:

1. Trace the historical development and philosophies of the three basic systems of government most common in the world today. List the reasons why the founders of the United States of America established a federal system of government, incorporating arguments both for and against federalism as it benefits the individual.

3. Differentiate among the constitutional powers (a) vested in the national government, (b) held by the states, and (c) shared by both, using national-government intervention in voting requirements as an example of reserved powers.

4. List the three most important clauses in the Constitution relating to "horizontal federalism," including the supremacy clause applied to the civil rights movement, and the full faith and credit clause applied to marriage and divorce.

5. Describe three milestones that have led to today's more powerful national government.

6. Illustrate forces that have tended to increase federal mandates, by describing two separate methods under which the national government allocates tax dollars to state and local governments.

7. Explain how national and state governments work together to solve some intergovernmental issues, and do not work together on others, using the interstate highway system and waste-management problems as examples.

Key Terms

Watch for these terms and pay particular attention to what each one means, as you follow the textbook and telelesson.

Unitary system	Supremacy clause
Confederal system	*McCulloch v. Maryland*
Federal system	*Gibbons v. Ogden*
"Elastic" ("necessary and proper") clause	Dual federalism
Horizontal federalism	Cooperative federalism
Full faith and credit clause	New federalism
Privileges and immunities	Federal mandates
Extradite	Categorical grants-in-aid
Interstate compacts	Project grant
	Block grants

Textbook Reading Assignment

Schmidt, Shelley, and Bardes. *American Government and Politics Today*, 1993-94 edition. Chapter 3, "Federalism," pp. 63-96.

Textbook Focus Points

Before you read the textbook assignment, review the following points to help focus your thoughts. After you complete the assignment, write out your responses to reinforce what you have learned.

1. What are the three basic systems of government, and which is the most common in the world today?

2. Why did its founders create a federal system of government for the United States of America?

---

3. What are the arguments for federalism?

4. What are the arguments against federalism?

5. What are the different types of power established in the Constitution?

6. What are the three most important clauses in the Constitution relating to "horizontal federalism"?

7. What three milestones have led to today's more powerful national government?

8. What are the three historical phases of federalism?

9. What are federal mandates, and what effect have they had on state and local governments?

10. What are two separate methods by which the national government returns tax dollars it collects to state and local governments?

Telelesson Interviewees

The following individuals share their expertise in the telelesson:

Richard Cole–Dean of Urban Studies, University of Texas, Arlington
Daniel J. Elazar–Director, Center for Study of Federalism, Temple University
Andy Hernandez–President, Southwest Voter Registration and Education Project
Eugene Jones–Professor of Government, Angelo State University
Mark McIntire–Environment Writer, *Newsday*, Long Island, N.Y.
J. Winston Porter–Assistant Administrator, U.S. Environmental Protection Agency

Telelesson Focus Points

Before viewing the telelesson, read over the following points to help focus your thoughts. After the presentation, write out your responses to help you remember these important points.

1. How was the supremacy clause of the Constitution applied to the civil rights movement?

2. What are "reserved powers"? How could the national government intervene in voting requirements, a power reserved to the states?

3. Explain the full faith and credit clause.

4. What role does federalism play in building the interstate highway system?

5. How does federalism benefit individuals?

6. What role does federalism play in dealing with the problem of trash?

7. According to the EPA, how can individuals become involved in solving today's waste-management problems?

Recommended Reading

The following suggestions are not required unless your instructor assigns them. They are listed to let you know where you can find additional information on areas which interest you.

Elazar, Daniel J. *American Federalism: A View from the States*. New York: Harper and Row, 1984.

Garreau, Joel. *The Nine Nations of North America*. New York: Avon Press, 1981.

Getting Involved

These activities are not required unless your instructor assigns them. But they offer good suggestions to help you understand and become more involved in the political process.

1. Write a two or three paragraph editorial on the nature of American federalism. Express your beliefs about American federalism, and cite what you believe should be the proper division of responsibility between the national government and the states in solving environmental problems such as pollution and sanitary landfills.

2. Pay close attention to news magazines, periodicals, and newspapers to find examples of continuing problems of federalism, the states versus the national government. Make a collage of these articles and write a brief summary on how you believe these problems could be solved.

3. Note the "Getting Involved" section in your textbook at the end of Chapter 3.

Self Test

After reading the assignment and watching the telelesson, you should be able to answer these questions. When you have completed the test, turn to the Answer Key to score your answers.

1. In a unitary system, the ultimate governmental authority is the
   a. national or central government.
   b. state or provincial government.
   c. local or city government.
   d. regional or multi-state government.

2. In a confederal political system, the central governing unit has power
   a. over state governments.
   b. over local governments.
   c. to make laws directly applicable to individuals only with approval of state governments.
   d. to revoke laws that are directly applicable to individuals only with the approval of state governments.

3. In a federal political system, power is
   a. always vested in a bicameral legislature.
   b. shared between the central government and constituent governments.
   c. vested only in the central government.
   d. concentrated in a unicameral legislature within a weak central government.

4. The people who wrote the Constitution created a federal system of government because the confederal system
   a. placed too many restrictions on the power of state governments.
   b. proved to be too weak to allow the government to face common problems.
   c. addressed primarily county-government authority in relationship to state governments.
   d. created a central government that developed too much power over the rights of individuals.

5. An advantage of federalism is that some governmental functions are
   a. farmed out to states or provinces.
   b. uniform throughout the country.
   c. decided by the central government.
   d. not allowed to be administered by any form of government lower than the state province.

6. An argument against federalism is that it provides a
   a. training ground for future national leaders.
   b. testing ground for new, bold, government initiatives.
   c. way for powerful states and local interests to block progress and impede national plans.
   d. method for local governments to sabotage the central government.

7. Most of the delegated powers of the national government involve the
   a. rights of the people.
   b. legislative branch.
   c. right of state-government approval.
   d. amendment process.

8. The implied powers of the national government
    a. are limited by decisions of state governments.
    b. are delegated in Article II, Section 6.
    c. give elasticity to our constitutional system.
    d. restrict Congress from passing legislation that is not specifically delegated in the Constitution.

9. The Tenth Amendment states that the powers not delegated to the United States by the Constitution, nor prohibited by it to the states, are reserved for the
    a. Congress.
    b. central government.
    c. states or the people.
    d. executive branch.

10. A major reason for the full faith and credit clause is to insure that
    a. rights established in contracts in one state will be honored by other states.
    b. laws passed by Congress will be enforced with full faith by state governments.
    c. contracts executed between the United States and another country will be honored.
    d. goods produced in one state will have priority over goods produced in another state.

11. The privileges and immunities clause of the Constitution means that
    a. elected officials of the national government cannot be tried by state governments.
    b. elected officials of state governments cannot be tried by the national government.
    c. citizens of one state cannot be treated as aliens in another state.
    d. citizens of another country cannot be treated as aliens in any state.

12. In the case of *McCulloch v. Maryland*, the Supreme Court ruled that a national bank could be established because the national government
    a. can expand its authority through expressed powers.
    b. can do whatever is needed in a time of crisis.
    c. has the expressed power to establish a bank.
    d. has those powers indispensable to the exercise of its designated powers.

13. The heart of the controversy that led to the Civil War was the issue of
    a. slavery.
    b. voting rights for ethnic minorities.
    c. national government supremacy versus rights of the separate states.
    d. whether or not there should be any more new slave states.

14. In the area of economic regulation, the legal doctrine of dual federalism emphasized the
    a. vast increase in the power of the national government.
    b. distinction between federal and state spheres of authority.
    c. role of the president in resolving major economic disputes.
    d. importance of the ability of state governments to limit the national government's power through amendments.

15. The goal of new federalism in relation to federal grants is to
    a. reduce the restrictions.
    b. increase the restrictions.
    c. reduce the role of state governments.
    d. increase the role of the federal government.

16. The requirements in federal legislation that force states to comply with certain rules are called
    a. matching funds.
    b. equalization factors.
    c. federal aids.
    d. federal mandates.

17. President Bush, in the 1992 State of the Union message, referred to the problem of federal mandates on the state and municipal governments and recommended that
    a. the president be given supervision over all federal mandates.
    b. state and local governments be authorized to supervise all federal mandates.
    c. federal mandates be declared unconstitutional.
    d. Congress be forced to pay for any federal mandate that it passes.

18. Federal grants-in-aid to states or local governments that are to be spent on specific programs or projects are called
    a. revenue-sharing funds.
    b. categorical grants.
    c. matching funds.
    d. equalization methods.

19. Block grants have grown slowly because
    a. state governors and mayors strongly oppose them.
    b. members of Congress have tried to impose them on the strongly opposed states.
    c. revenue sharing programs depleted grant funds before block grant applications could be reviewed.
    d. their supports are too diffused to force Congress to increase them.

20. With the passage of the Civil Rights Act of 1964, the supremacy clause of the U.S. Constitution allowed the courts to declare
    a. unconstitutional all federal laws that disallowed discrimination.
    b. unconstitutional all state laws that disallowed discrimination.
    c. constitutional all federal laws that permitted or mandated discrimination.
    d. unconstitutional state laws that permitted or mandated discrimination.

21. Even though states have the right to set voting requirements through their reserved powers granted by the Constitution, the national government intervened by passing Voting Rights Acts to
    a. conduct all federal elections.
    b. redesign confusing ballots.
    c. allocate large sums to register voters.
    d. remove barriers that confronted minorities when voting or registering to vote.

22. Article 4 of the Constitution and clauses like full faith and credit insure that all states will
    a. honor the rules, laws, regulations, and court decisions of every other state.
    b. place the same value on all the currencies of each state.
    c. transfer the credit ratings of individuals to each state in which they live.
    d. show the same amount of faith in all minority groups as is shown in whites.

23. The construction and maintenance of the interstate highway system is an example of federalism in which the states
    a. blocked the federal government from building state highways.
    b. maintained control over the construction.
    c. joined the national government to solve a problem.
    d. financed the major portion of the highway construction.

24. Federalism permits individuals to
    a. go from state to state without needing a passport.
    b. affect government at different levels by providing many points of access.
    c. attend colleges all over the country in order to obtain a well-rounded education.
    d. borrow money from all levels of government.

25. The problem of waste management is an example of federalism in which the states and the national government have
    a. been unable to join together to solve a problem satisfactorily.
    b. very few problems in reaching a satisfactory agreement.
    c. agreed that the states should solve a local problem.
    d. refused to finance expensive waste-disposal plants.

26. Individuals can help in solving waste-management problems by understanding local regulations and by
    a. delivering their own trash to the landfill in plastic bags.
    b. separating various kinds of garbage for recycling.
    c. digging a large hole in their backyards to bury trash.
    d. contributing money to campaigns to enlarge incinerators.

Short-Answer Question:
27. In a brief paragraph, describe what you expect will happen with federalism in the United States during the next decade.

Answer Key

These are the correct answers with reference to the Learning Objectives, and to the source of the information: the Textbook Focus Points, Schmidt, *et al. American Government and Politics Today* (Schmidt), and the Telelesson Focus Points. Page numbers are also given for the Textbook Focus Points. "KT" indicates questions with Key Terms defined.

Question	Answer	Learning Objective	Textbook Focus Point (page no.)		Telelesson Focus Point
1	A	1	1 (Schmidt, pp. 65-66)	KT	
2	C	1	1 (Schmidt, p. 66)	KT	
3	B	1	1 (Schmidt, p. 66)	KT	
4	B	2	2 (Schmidt, p. 67)	KT	
5	A	2	3 (Schmidt, p. 71)		
6	C	2	4 (Schmidt, p. 73)		
7	B	3	5 (Schmidt, p. 73)		
8	C	3	5 (Schmidt, p. 73)		
9	C	3	5 (Schmidt, p. 75)		
10	A	4	6 (Schmidt, p. 78)	KT	3
11	C	4	6 (Schmidt, p. 78)	KT	
12	D	5	7 (Schmidt, p. 81)	KT	
13	C	5	7 (Schmidt, p. 82)		
14	B	1	8 (Schmidt, p. 86)	KT	
15	A	1	8 (Schmidt, pp. 88-89)	KT	
16	D	6	9 (Schmidt, p. 90)	KT	
17	D	6	9 (Schmidt, p. 92)	KT	
18	B	6	10 (Schmidt, p. 90)	KT	
19	D	6	10 (Schmidt, p. 91)	KT	
20	D	4			1
21	D	3			2
22	A	4			3
23	C	7			4
24	B	2			5
25	A	7			6
26	B	7			7

Short Answer:

27		7			4,5,6

Local Government

Overview

A previous lesson on federalism introduced the concept of different levels of government. Keep in mind throughout this lesson that the U.S. Constitution makes no mention of local governments; it only speaks of national and state governments. Consequently, under the Constitution every local government is a creature of the state.

Yet many government scholars believe that local government may be the most important layer of government as far as the individual is concerned, because local government affects our daily lives much more than state and national governments. The quality of our police and fire protection, the condition of the streets, the purity of our water, the frequency and method of trash collection, the availability of parks and playgrounds, the choices and conditions of medical services, the quality of our public schools, and many other rules and services all are determined by local governments.

In most states local government consists basically of cities, counties, and special districts. In this lesson we briefly examine how states and their local governments raise and spend their revenues, then look at the major types of municipal governments.

We then focus on two cities: Chicago, Illinois, and Richardson, Texas; the former a city in the center of a major urban area and the latter a suburban city. Each had a different problem, but both local governments were influenced by individuals who organized at the grass-roots level to disprove the adage that "you can't fight city hall." The two examples also illustrate how important it is for us to know how local governments operate, for this is the government that affects each one of us on a daily basis.

Learning Objectives

Goal: The purpose of "Local Government" is to describe the various kinds of local governments and to present examples of how ordinary individuals can impact decisions made at the local level.

Objectives:

1. Identify the primary sources of raising revenue for state and local government, emphasizing differences in income taxing systems.

2. Explain the different types of local governments (municipal, county, state, and special districts), including legal status, establishment and interaction, major functions, and important issues.

3. Describe the four basic plans which govern municipalities.

4. Provide general examples of ways that individuals are affected by local governments and can make changes in local governments.

5. Compare the effects of "grass roots" organization in Richardson, Texas, and Chicago, Illinois, including the issue, the actions taken, and the relative success of each.

Key Terms

Watch for these terms and pay particular attention to what each one means, as you follow the textbook and telelesson.

General sales tax	Special districts
Property tax	Councils of governments (COGs)
Home rule city	Commission plan
General law city	Council-manager plan
Municipalities	Mayor-council plan
County	Patronage

Textbook Reading Assignment

Schmidt, Shelley, and Bardes. *American Government and Politics Today*, 1993-94 edition. Chapter 19, "State and Local Government," pp. 631-638, 650-662.

Textbook Focus Points

Before you read the textbook assignment, review the following points to help focus your thoughts. After you complete the assignment, write out your responses to reinforce what you have learned.

1. What are the primary sources of revenue for state governments and for local governments?

2. How was the legal existence of local government established?

3. What are the basic types of local governments?

4. Describe the four basic plans by which municipalities are governed.

Telelesson Interviewees

The following individuals share their expertise in the telelesson:

Mark Atkinson–Former President, C.U.B.S. (Citizens United for Baseball in the Sunshine), Chicago, Illinois
Rod Bond–Leader, Homeowners Association, Richardson, Texas
Bernard Hanson–Alderman, 44th Ward, Chicago, Illinois
William J. McCoy–Director, Urban Institute, University of North Carolina, Charlotte
Charles L. Spann–Mayor, Richardson, Texas

Telelesson Focus Points

Before viewing the telelesson, read over the following points to help focus your thoughts. After the presentation, write out your responses to help you remember these important points.

1. To what extent can individuals influence local government?

2. What was the issue that caused the citizens of Richardson, Texas, to "fight City Hall"?

3. What did the citizens of Richardson do to influence their local government? Evaluate their success.

4. What was the problem between Chicago's powerful Tribune Company and the neighborhood of "Wrigleyville"?

5. How did Chicago's local government resolve the problem between "Wrigleyville" and the Tribune Company? Evaluate the success of the "Wrigleyville" community in influencing their local government.

6. According to William McCoy, what is "nimby," and how does it motivate people to get involved in local government?

Recommended Reading

The following suggestions are not required unless your instructor assigns them. They are listed to let you know where you can find additional information on areas which interest you.

Banfield, Edward C. and Wilson, James Q. *City Politics*. New York: Vintage Books, 1963.

Royko, Mike. *Boss: Richard J. Daley of Chicago*. New York: New American Library, 1971.

Getting Involved

These activities are not required unless your instructor assigns them. But they offer good suggestions to help you understand and become more involved in the political process.

1. Attend a meeting of your city or town council. Write a paragraph about your observations of the meeting, such as the issues addressed and the participation of citizens.

2. Read your local newspaper to find activities of the levels of local government under which you live: city, county, and special districts. Collect these articles, and write a paragraph about how the activities affect you and what you could do to influence these actions.

3. Note the "Getting Involved" section in your textbook at the end of Chapter 19.

Self Test

After reading the assignment and watching the telelesson, you should be able to answer these questions. When you have completed the test, turn to the Answer Key to score your answers.

1. By far the most important tax at the state level is the
   a. gasoline tax.
   b. property tax.
   c. general sales tax.
   d. car-tag tax.

2. In most parts of the United States the most important tax at the local level is the
   a. gasoline tax.
   b. property tax.
   c. general sales tax.
   d. car-tag tax.

3. Every local government is a creature of
   a. the state.
   b. the national government.
   c. a special district.
   d. a county government.

4. Local governments that spend their revenues primarily to provide water and other utilities, as well as police and fire protection, are called
   a. special districts.
   b. counties.
   c. municipalities.
   d. town halls.

5. The primary government set up by the state to administer state law at the local level is the
   a. special district.
   b. county.
   c. municipality.
   d. home-rule city.

6. The form of local government found in largest numbers is the
   a. municipality.
   b. county.
   c. township.
   d. special district.

7. In the commission plan of city government, vesting both legislative and executive power in the hands of a small group means that there will be
   a. no checks and balances on administration and spending.
   b. a short ballot when the commissioners are elected.
   c. no need for a mayor or speaker of the house.
   d. no need for a partisan election.

8. Having no single, strong, political leader is a major defect of both the commission plan and the
   a. strong mayor-council plan.
   b. weak mayor-council plan.
   c. patronage plan.
   d. council-manager plan.

9. In the strong mayor-council plan, the mayor is
   a. a poorly-paid executive.
   b. responsible for all the activities related to health care.
   c. an elected executive who may appoint department heads.
   d. no longer a member of the council.

10. Local government is an easily influenced level of government because
    a. the president would rather visit constituents in their homes.
    b. a small fraction of the population can bring about enormous change.
    c. members of the House and Senate like to visit their home states.
    d. hometown problems are less complex and easier to solve.

11. Homeowners in Richardson, Texas, were outraged because a proposed construction project would
    a. require additional buses from the mass-transit system.
    b. destroy the public parks where their children played.
    c. hire laborers from outside the city.
    d. bring additional cars to an already busy neighborhood.

12. The citizens of Richardson, Texas, influenced their local government first by circulating a petition to oppose the construction project and finally by
    a. contacting the members of Congress from their district.
    b. buying radio spots to announce a "town hall" meeting.
    c. running candidates for the council seats that were up for election.
    d. requesting help from neighboring suburbs.

13. The citizens of Richardson, Texas, were partially successful in the zoning case, but they were very successful in gaining control of city government by
    a. electing a majority of the members of the city council.
    b. defeating the builder who was also mayor.
    c. hiring a new city manager.
    d. gaining a seat on all city boards and commissions.

14. The residents of "Wrigleyville" were proud of their "Cubbies" and wanted the Tribune Company to
    a. buy new uniforms for their team.
    b. put artificial turf on the stadium field.
    c. leave the stadium and team unchanged.
    d. install a sprinkler system for the field.

15. To fight the installation of lights at Wrigley Field, the neighborhood residents
    a. threatened to shoot out the lights.
    b. tried to raise funds to buy the stadium.
    c. contacted the mayor and tried to persuade him to oppose the lights.
    d. formed a group called "Citizens United for Baseball in the Sunshine" (CUBS).

16. When night-time baseball finally came to Wrigley field, the residents of "Wrigleyville" were successful in
    a. selling their properties for parking lots.
    b. limiting the number of night games.
    c. collecting a percentage of the gate receipts.
    d. having a monopoly on the concessions.

17. The thing that motivates people to get involved in local government probably more than anything else is
    a. some direct action by local government that impacts them.
    b. the feeling of contributing to the community good.
    c. a strong sense of patriotic duty.
    d. the chance to gain control of government for a sense of power.

Short-Answer Question:

18. If your neighborhood encountered problems similar to those in Richardson and Chicago, what measures would you recommend? Write a paragraph outlining your suggestions of ways to influence your own local government.

Answer Key

These are the correct answers with reference to the Learning Objectives, and to the source of the information: the Textbook Focus Points, Schmidt, *et al. American Government and Politics Today* (Schmidt), and the Telelesson Focus Points. Page numbers are also given for the Textbook Focus Points. "KT" indicates questions with Key Terms defined.

Question	Answer	Learning Objective	Text Focus Point (page no.)		Telelesson Focus Point
1.	C	1	1(Schmidt, p. 634)	KT	
2.	B	1	1 (Schmidt, p. 634)	KT	
3.	A	2	2 (Schmidt, p. 650)		
4.	C	2	3 (Schmidt, p. 651)	KT	
5.	B	2	3 (Schmidt, p. 651)	KT	
6.	D	2	4 (Schmidt, p. 654)	KT	
7.	A	3	4 (Schmidt, pp. 656-657)	KT	
8.	D	3	4 (Schmidt, p. 657)	KT	1
9.	C	3	4 (Schmidt, p. 657)	KT	1
10.	B	4			1
11.	D	5			2
12.	C	5			3
13.	A	5			3
14.	C	5			4
15.	D	5			5
16.	B	5			5
17.	A	4			6

Short Answer:

18.		4	3,5,6

Lesson 6

Political Participation

Overview

This lesson on "Political Participation" is the heart of this course, because its goal is for each of us to understand that it is possible for us, as concerned individuals, to make a difference in our community, our state, and our nation. By the same token, we must be aware of the consequences if too many of us become apathetic and don't take advantage of these opportunities, which basically are unique to a democratic society.

This lesson begins a series of lessons that deal, in one way or another, with the various means we can use to take part in the political process: participating through group activity such as with an interest group, participating in party politics at any of several levels, or participating in a campaign as a candidate or volunteer. Each kind of political participation is essential to the political process.

In the telelesson we hear from individuals like you and me, who see the importance of participating and do so in various ways—from joining a political party, writing letters to newspaper editors, or being willing to run for office and serve as an elected official within the political system, to working outside of the traditional system. We talk with members of a neighborhood organization, ACORN, and learn how one neighborhood achieves representation itself and brings about needed changes. Finally, we visit with a college professor who has studied another form of participation, voting, and find out why some people don't vote.

If you believe, as too many Americans do, that you don't have the time to become involved, or that participating in the political process is too much trouble, remember the words of Pastor Martin Neimoller, who fought against the rise of Adolf Hitler: "In Germany, they first came for the Communists and I didn't speak up because I wasn't a Communist. Then they came for the Jews, and I didn't speak up because I wasn't a Jew. They came for the trade unionists, and I didn't speak up because I wasn't a trade unionist. Then they came for the Catholics, and I didn't speak up because I was a Protestant. Then they came for me, and by that time no one was left to speak up."

Learning Objectives

Goal: The purpose of "Political Participation" is to illustrate why some citizens participate in the political system and others do not, and to emphasize why political participation is so vital to a free political system.

Objectives:

1. List the most important influences in the political-socialization process of our diverse society and describe why the process is not blocked by conflict and dissension.

2. Describe how government responds to public opinion, how individuals react to public opinion polls, and how labels are used to identify political candidates, office holders, and issues.

3. Compare voter turnout and registration patterns in the United States with those of other countries also having representative democratic governments.

4. Describe the factors that influence whether or not a person votes, and explain the processes individuals use to decide how they will vote.

5. List the requirements for voter registration, and explain why the requirements are needed.

---

6. Define political participation, and describe how an individual can participate inside and outside the traditional political system using ACORN and Tom Hayden as examples.

7. Explain why individuals don't get involved in the political process, and describe the costs and benefits of participating and not participating.

Key Terms

Watch for these terms and pay particular attention to what each one means, as you follow the textbook and telelesson.

Political socialization	Voter turnout
Liberal	Representative democratic government
Opinion leaders	Franchise
Political culture	Registration
Liberals	Socioeconomic status
Conservatives	Issue voting
Moderates	Political participation (TV)
Ideologue	ACORN (TV)

Textbook Readng Assignment

Schmidt, Shelley, and Bardes. *American Government and Politics Today*, 1993-94 edition. Chapter 7, "Public Opinion," pp. 209-238, and Chapter 10, "Campaigns, Candidates, and Elections," pp. 325-343.

Textbook Focus Points

Before you read the textbook assignment, review the following points to help focus your thoughts. After you complete the assignment, write out your responses to reinforce what you have learned.

1. What are the most important influences in the political-socialization process?

2. With the diversity of American society and its opinions, what prevents the political process from being blocked by conflict and dissension?

3. What has research shown about government response to public opinion?

4. How are political candidates and office holders frequently identified, and what issues does each "label" support?

5. How should an individual react to a public opinion poll?

6. What reasons are given for low voter turnout in a representative democratic government?

7. Compare voter turnout in the U.S. with voter turnout in other nations.

8. What factors influence whether or not a person votes?

9. What is required to register to vote, and why are these requirements needed?

10. How do voters decide to vote for particular candidates or issues?

11. What problems result from low levels of information?

Telelesson Interviewees

The following individuals share their expertise in the telelesson:

ACORN–Members of the Organization
Tommy Denton–Editorial Page Editor, *Ft. Worth Star Telegram*
Tom Hayden–Democrat; California State Assembly
Corrine Kehoe–Volunteer, Republican Party
Joseph Lieberman–Democrat; U.S. Senator, Connecticut
Frances Fox-Pivens–Professor of American Politics, Graduate School,
   City University of New York
John Pouland–Former Chair, Dallas County (Texas) Democratic
   Party
Peggy Rudd–Citizen Activist
Mike Synar–Democrat; U.S. Representative, Oklahoma
Deborah Wood–Volunteer, Democratic Party
David E. Wright–Dallas Rescue, Dallas, Texas

Telelesson Focus Points

Before viewing the telelesson, read over the following points to help
focus your thoughts. After the presentation, write out your responses
to help you remember these important points.

1. What is political participation, and how can an individual take
   part in politics?

2. Why do some people choose to participate outside the traditional
   system?

3. What is ACORN, and how has it accomplished its goals?

4. According to Frances Fox-Pivens, why don't more Americans
   vote and get involved?

5. What are the costs and benefits of political participation and
   non-participation?

Recommended Reading

The following suggestions are not required unless your instructor assigns them. They are listed to let you know where you can find additional information on areas which interest you.

Gans, Curtis. "Why Young People Don't Vote." *Education Digest* (February 1989): pp. 40-43.

Gordon, Charles. "With Lazy Voters, Who Needs Issues?" *Macleans* (November 7, 1988): p. 58.

Pivens, Frances Fox, and Richard A. Cloward. *Why Americans Don't Vote*. New York: Pantheon, 1988.

Smith, Gerald W., and Jerry Debenham. "Intelligent Voting Systems: Using Computers for Choosing Our Leaders." *The Futurist* 22 (Sept./Oct. 1988): pp. 38-42.

Teixeira, Ruy A. *Why Americans Don't Vote: Turnout Decline in the United States, 1960-1984*. New York: Greenwood Press, 1987.

Getting Involved

These activities are not required unless your instructor assigns them. But they offer good suggestions to help you understand and become more involved in the political process.

1. Note the "Getting Involved" section of your textbook at the end of Chapter 10.

2. Read the "Letters to the Editor" section of local newspapers. Figure out which issues generate the greatest individual response.

3. Find a current issue or incident about which you hold a strong opinion, and write a letter to the editor of your local newspaper expressing that opinion.

4. Analyze your own opinions on matters of public interest. Try to determine the sources which have had the greatest impact in shaping your opinions–family, friends, job, television.

5. Figure out whether you would categorize yourself as a liberal, conservative, or moderate. Write out the reasons why you put yourself in that category.

Self Test

After reading the assignment and watching the telelesson, you should be able to answer these questions. When you have completed the test, turn to the Answer Key to score your answers.

1. Most views expressed as political opinions are acquired
   a. just before polls are conducted.
   b. through a process known as political socialization.
   c. from ideas that appear as questions in public opinion polls.
   d. outside the current political culture.

2. Two of the strongest influences in shaping the opinions of Americans are
   a. the media and peers.
   b. opinion leaders and religion.
   c. education and gender.
   d. race and income.

3. Which of the following is NOT part of a set of key values in our political culture that prevents the American political process from being blocked by conflict and dissension?
   a. Life, liberty, and property
   b. Universal suffrage
   c. Religious beliefs
   d. High value on community service and personal achievement

4. In terms of government responsiveness to public opinion, research suggests that the national government responds
   a. rarely to public opinion.
   b. to changes in public opinion about two-thirds of the time.
   c. seldom to public opinion because of the structure of that government.
   d. to opinion polls for shaping public policy.

5. The ideological position of political candidates and officeholders in the United States are frequently identified as
   a. leftists or rightists.
   b. Democrats or Republicans.
   c. liberals or conservatives.
   d. capitalists or socialists.

6. In evaluating a public opinion poll, the first question we should ask is:
   a. How much did the poll cost?
   b. Who conducted the poll?
   c. How will the poll be used?
   d. How was the poll sample selected?

7. One major reason for low voter turnout in elections is that a majority of the adult population
   a. does not understand simple facts regarding the political process.
   b. does not know the candidates for most elective positions.
   c. cannot pass the basic voter-registration test.
   d. refuses to pay the property tax which can be a prerequisite for registration.

8. The voter turnout in the United States, compared with that of other western democracies, places the United States in
   a. last place.
   b. the bottom 20 percent.
   c. the top half.
   d. first place.

9. One reason people vote is the
   a. chance to be excused from jury duty.
   b. homestead exemption received on their personal property tax.
   c. privilege of obtaining a passport without questions.
   d. personal satisfaction they receive from the act of voting.

10. Which of the following is NOT a requirement for voter registration?
    a. Pay a poll tax
    b. Be a citizen
    c. Reach age 18
    d. Reside in state

11. Which of the following factors does NOT influence voting decisions?
    a. Demographic
    b. Socioeconomic
    c. Psychological
    d. Meteorological

12. Which of the following socioeconomic classes tends to vote Republican?
    a. Manual laborers and factory workers
    b. Professionals and business people
    c. Union members and women
    d. Contract laborers and artisans

13. The poorly informed vote less and the better informed have higher turnout because of
    a. low information levels and interest.
    b. high information levels and no interest.
    c. high interest and no information.
    d. television coverage and newspaper fraud.

14. The activities of individuals that help determine who their political leaders will be, who runs the government, and what that government does are called:
    a. pocketbook voting.
    b. political participation.
    c. political polling.
    d. representative government.

15. Some people operate outside the traditional political system because they do NOT
    a. understand how the system operates.
    b. have the financial support to join it.
    c. believe that the system is accessible to them.
    d. know who the leaders are.

16. The community-based organization that grew out of the welfare rights movement of the '60s and concentrates its efforts at the neighborhood level is known as
    a. NAACP.
    b. CREEP.
    c. SEATO.
    d. ACORN.

17. According to political scientist and author Frances Fox-Pivens, Americans don't get involved in their government because they
    a. are too involved in their daily lives and don't want to give up their leisure time.
    b. view the American system of voter registration as putting the burden of registering on the individual.
    c. believe that most politicians are crooks and don't want to support a corrupt system.
    d. judge the American system to be fragmented and too costly to operate efficiently.

Short-Answer Question:

18. Discuss the costs and benefits of political participation and non-participation, keeping in mind Pastor Martin Neimoller's words.

Answer Key

These are the correct answers with reference to the Learning Objectives, and to the source of the information: the Textbook Focus Points, Schmidt, *et al. American Government and Politics Today* (Schmidt), and the Telelesson Focus Points. Page numbers are also given for the Textbook Focus Points. "KT" indicates questions with Key Terms defined.

Question	Answer	Learning Objective	Textbook Focus Point (page no.)	Telelesson Focus Point
1	B	1	1 (Schmidt, p. 223)....KT	
2	D	1	1 (Schmidt, p. 229)	
3	B	1	2 (Schmidt, p. 231)	
4	B	2	3 (Schmidt, p. 234)	
5	C	2	4 (Schmidt, p. 234)....KT	
6	D	2	5 (Schmidt, p. 237)	
7	A	3	6 (Schmidt, p. 329)....KT	
8	B	3	7 (Schmidt, p. 326)....KT	
9	D	4	8 (Schmidt, p. 330)	
10	A	5	9 (Schmidt, p. 333)....KT	
11	D	4	10 (Schmidt, p. 334)	
12	B	4	10 (Schmidt, p. 336)	
13	A	4	11 (Schmidt, p. 331)	
14	B	6		1
15	C	6		2
16	D	6		3
17	B	7		4

Short Answer:

18		7		5

NRA Fact Sheet

What is the Gun Lobby?
un Lobby is People.

1978 general elections, the NRA-
close to one million dollars in
with members, in direct
or in independent
1980, it spent an
elections saw
-year

AARP NEWS

For further inquiry, contact American Association of Retired Persons • Office of Communications
1909 K Street, N.W. • Washington, DC 20049 • (202) 728-4300

FACT SHEET

AARP -- the American Association of Retired Persons -- is a nonprofit, nonpartisan organization dedicated to helping older Americans achieve lives of independence, dignity and purpose.

Founded in 1958 by the late Dr. Ethel Percy Andrus, AARP is today the nation's oldest and largest organization of older Americans, with a membership of more than 28 million. Membership is open to anyone age 50 or older, whether working or retired. One-third of the Association's membership is made up of older workers.

P's motto is "to serve, not to be served." Members give ning to that motto through involvement in community, st onal affairs.

ERSHIP

dent -- Mrs. Louise C
ive Director

Lesson 7

Interest Groups

Overview

A previous lesson defined political participation and described how each of us can participate. This lesson narrows the focus to a specific way in which we can take part in the political process: joining an interest group.

Perhaps Americans have always been joiners, for George Washington warned against the formation of factions in American politics. As early as 1834, Alexis de Tocqueville noted the joining nature of Americans. Throughout U.S. history, we have based our freedom to join, and to speak out, on the constitutional guarantees of freedom of speech, assembly, and petition.

Today most of us are members of several organizations, either for social or professional reasons. But interest groups hold a special place in the American political process, since they provide us with an opportunity to join with others who share our political ideas, beliefs, and opinions, in order to influence the actions of our government.

A previous lesson revealed how important it is for each of us to participate in the governmental process. This lesson focuses on one way to do this, by becoming a member of a politically active interest group, and shows us how these operate within the American political system.

First, we examine the two basic categories of interest groups: broad focus and narrow focus. We choose one organization to represent each category (broad focus: AARP, and narrow focus: NRA) and investigate their goals, methods of operation, successes, and failures. We also hear from representatives of each group.

Next, we look briefly at another category: the single-issue interest group. These groups differ from the two major types because they are even more focused, disciplined, and highly committed, with just one reason for existing. Single-issue interest groups are becoming more visible in today's politics; chances are that you have spotted some of their causes on bumper stickers.

The key to success for any interest group is its ability to have access to government offices. To achieve this, interest groups must develop strategies; one of the better known strategies is lobbying. Most of us have heard about lobbying abuses, but today's lobbyists can be valuable resources in providing expert information for our elected officials.

Another strategy that increases an interest group's ability to reach key people in government is forming political action committees (PACs), which provide financial resources for many elected officials. Because another lesson focuses on PACs, we only introduce them here. Other lessons go into more detail about additional ways of participating in the political process, including PACs, the media, and political parties.

Learning Objectives

Goal: The purpose of "Interest Groups" is to demonstrate the importance of interest groups in the political system, by showing how such organizations influence policy-making by government officials.

Objectives:

1. Construct a definition of the political entity called interest groups, covering types, constitutional basis, roles, functions, and examples of these groups.

2. Tell how individual members affect interest groups, and what techniques interest groups use to achieve their objectives.

3. Describe the role of the lobbyist as an interest-group representative and how the government attempts to regulate lobbyists.

4. Outline the reasons why interest groups have grown so powerful and the ways in which they influence the policy-making process.

5. Describe the focus and success of two interest groups: the broad-focused American Association of Retired Persons (AARP) and the narrow-focus
ed National Rifle Association (NRA).

Key Terms

Watch for these terms and pay particular attention to what each one means, as you follow the textbook and telelesson.

Interest group	Political action committees(PACs)
Public interest	Grass roots tactics
Direct techniques	Rifle technique
Indirect techniques	*Amicus curiae*(TV)
Lobbying	Single-issue interest groups(TV)

Textbook Reading Assignment

Schmidt, Shelley, and Bardes. *American Government and Politics Today*, 1993-94 edition. Chapter 8, "Interest Groups," pp. 239-265.

Textbook Focus Points

Before you read the textbook assignment, review the following points to help focus your thoughts. After you complete the assignment, write out your responses to reinforce what you have learned.

1. What is an interest group, and into what major classifications do interest groups fall?

2. What is the logic behind Mancur Olson's theory of collective action?

3. What are some techniques that interest groups use to achieve their goals?

4. What is meant by "high-tech lobbying"?

5. How are lobbyists regulated?

6. Why do interest groups have so much power?

Telelesson Interviewees

The following individuals share their expertise in the telelesson:

Steve Bartlett–Republican; Former U.S. Representative, Texas
Paul Blackman–Assistant Director of Research and Information, National Rifle Association (NRA)
John C. Rother–Director of Legislation, Research, and Public Policy Division; American Association of Retired People (AARP)
Pamela Sederholm–Government Affairs Consultant

Telelesson Focus Points

Before viewing the telelesson, read over the following points to help focus your thoughts. After the presentation, write out your responses to help you remember these important points.

1. What are interest groups, and what is the constitutional basis for them?

2. How do interest groups take action?

3. What does a lobbyist do?

4. What are the two major categories of interest groups, and what do they emphasize?

5. What is the focus of the American Association of Retired Persons (AARP), and how does it try to influence government?

6. What is the focus of the National Rifle Association (NRA), and why is it so successful as an interest group?

7. What is a single-issue interest group, and what tactics does such a group use to influence government?

Recommended Reading

The following suggestions are not required unless your instructor assigns them. They are listed to let you know where you can find additional information on areas which interest you.

Evans, Rowland, and Robert D Novack. "Washington's Shameful Revolving Door." *Reader's Digest* 130 (May 1987): pp. 118-120.

Foley, Thomas J. "When Interest Groups Grade Lawmakers." *U.S. News & World Report* 98 (June 10, 1985): p. 50.

Karmin, Monroe W. "When Special Interests Draw Bead on Law Reform."*U.S. News & World Report* 98 (February 25, 1985): pp. 22-24.

Thomas, Evan. "Peddling Influence."*Time* 127 (March 3, 1986) :pp 126-130+.

Getting Involved

These activities are not required unless your instructor assigns them. But they offer good suggestions to help you understand and become more involved in the political process.

1. Note the "Getting Involved" section of your textbook at the end of Chapter 8.

2. Make a list of all the interest groups with which you are associated. Why have you chosen to be a part of them? In what way (or ways) does each represent an interest of yours?

Self Test

After reading the assignment and watching the telelesson, you should be able to answer these questions. When you have completed the test, turn to the Answer Key to score your answers.

1. An interest group is any organization that
   a. provides interesting information to its members.
   b. consists of people who want control of the government.
   c. actively attempts to influence government policy-makers.
   d. requires members to pay dues before they can participate.

2. Three of the most influential types of interest groups in the United States are
   a. ideological, philosophical, and governmental.
   b. liberal, pro-abortion, and foreign-policy isolationist.
   c. business, agriculture, and labor.
   d. teachers, state governments, and homeowners.

3. According to the theory of Mancur Olson, it is simply not rational fo individuals to
   a. join most interest groups.
   b. avoid participation within a dominant political party.
   c. belong to a political party and not vote a straight party ballot.
   d. pay union dues.

4. The key to success for an interest group is the
    a. collection of dues from its members.
    b. number of lobbyists it employs in Washington, D.C.
    c. ability to have access to governmental officials.
    d. size of its donations to political campaigns.

5. One particularly important aspect of lobbying in this new era of interest-group activity is
    a. the formation of an information bank to which all interest groups can have access.
    b. for each interest group to have a well-staffed and well-equipped Washington, D.C., office.
    c. recruiting college graduates to research topics and input the information on computers for later use.
    d. the use of modern high-technology to enhance the role of pressure groups.

6. A problem facing Congress in attempting to apply stricter regulation to lobbying is the
    a. lack of money that interest groups have to spend on lobbying.
    b. constitutional problem of abridging First Amendment rights.
    c. need for lobbyists to provide the legislators with more research.
    d. lack of power that interest groups have with elected officials.

7. Interest groups are successful, in part, due to the
    a. structure of American government.
    b. small number of interest groups.
    c. strong, responsive, political-party system.
    d. large number of emotional issues.

8. Interest groups do NOT base their existence on the guaranteed constitutional right of freedom
    a. to speak.
    b. to bear arms.
    c. to assemble.
    d. to petition.

---

9. Interest groups do NOT take action by
    a. using political action committees to raise funds for members.
    b. urging members to work for the election of particular individuals.
    c. influencing various agencies within the executive branch.
    d. selecting some of their members to run for public office.

10. Which of the following is NOT a role of lobbyists?
    a. To learn everything about the organization they work for
    b. To provide elected officials with well-staffed offices
    c. To make elected officials aware of what the issues are
    d. To give elected officials accurate facts and figures

11. The two major categories of interest groups are
    a. broad focus and narrow focus.
    b. special interest and single interest.
    c. business and agriculture.
    d. large membership and small membership.

12. Because it caters to more than just its members' political concerns, AARP
    a. has a number of professional lobbyists.
    b. has a small membership.
    c. is a narrow-focus interest group.
    d. is a broad-focus interest group.

13. The NRA is a very effective interest group because it has
    a. a claim of constitutional protection and appeals to a very broad-focused group of individuals.
    b. the support of established corporations and a professional staff that specializes in sportsmanship.
    c. professional lobbyists in Washington, D.C., and a watchful, dedicated membership ready to respond.
    d. a large membership that can raise large sums, and a broad-focused concentration on the issues.

14. Single-issue interest groups are those groups with
    a. a single minority-group membership.
    b. just one reason for being.
    c. broader focus than the NRA.
    d. little commitment to one issue.

Short-Answer Question:

15. How can individuals impact an interest group?

Answer Key

These are the correct answers with reference to the Learning Objectives, and to the source of the information: the Textbook Focus Points, Schmidt, *et al. American Government and Politics Today* (Schmidt), and the Telelesson Focus Points. Page numbers are also given for the Textbook Focus Points. "KT" indicates questions with Key Terms defined.

Question	Answer	Learning Objective	Textbook Focus Point (page no.)		Telelesson Focus Point
1	C	1	1 (Schmidt, p. 241)	KT	
2	C	1	1 (Schmidt, p. 244)		
3	A	2	2 (Schmidt, p. 250)		
4	C	2	3 (Schmidt, p. 253)	KT	
5	D	2	4 (Schmidt, p. 259)		
6	B	3	5 (Schmidt, pp. 261-262)	KT	
7	A	4	6 (Schmidt, p. 262)		
8	B	1			1
9	D	2			2
10	B	3			3
11	A	1			4
12	D	5			5
13	C	5			6
14	B	1		KT	7

Short Answer:

15		2	2 (Schmidt, pp. 252-253)		7

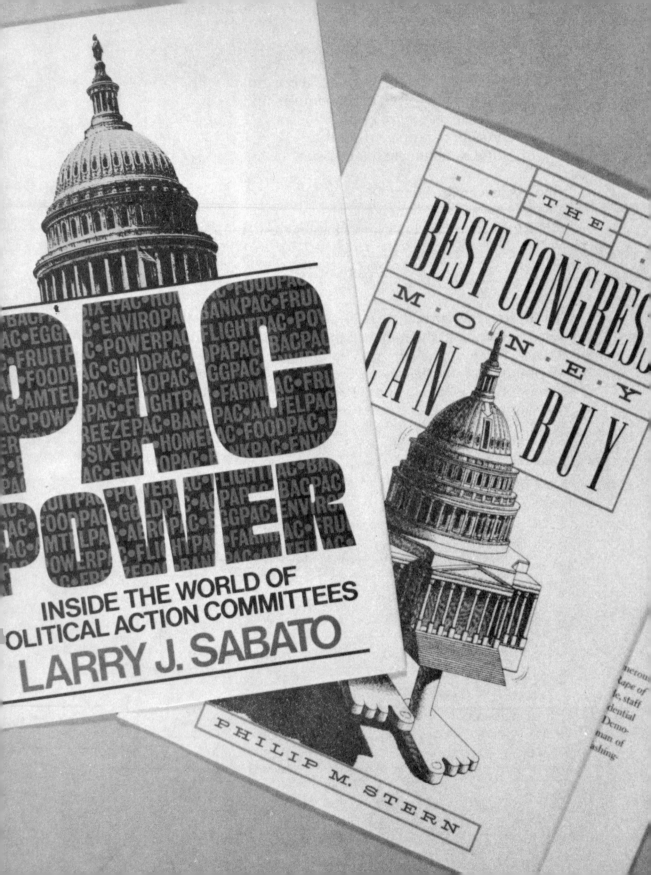

Lesson 8

The Power of PACs

Overview

In 1974 Congress passed the Federal Election Campaign Act, which severely restricts the amount of money any one individual can donate to a federal campaign. It also prohibits interest groups and corporations from making direct donations to candidates or their campaigns.

However, this Act, and amendments to it passed in 1976, also spells out specific guidelines under which candidates may legitimately receive campaign funds. Out of this legislation grew a new phenomenon, called political action committees. PACs were formed so that, by following precise rules, these groups could contribute to candidates on behalf of their interest group, corporation, or labor union.

Today, however, the power that political action committees wield has grown awesome. If properly used, the money furnished by PACs can be an appropriate part of our democratic process. But the probability for abuse of the PAC system is very real.

Because political action committees are creations of interest groups, corporations, or labor unions, this lesson on "The Power of PACs" builds on the ideas presented in a previous lesson on interest groups. Here we define PACs and examine their reason for existence. At the same time we note that some observers of our political system fear that PACs will destroy our representative form of government, in part because members of Congress may be more responsive to the blocks of people who make these large campaign contributions than to the individual constituents who actually elect the members of Congress.

During the 1987-88 election, PACs put 74 percent of their money on incumbents. This explains another criticism or fear about PACs: that challengers will find financing a campaign so costly and difficult that fewer people will be willing or financially able to challenge an incumbent. This lack of electoral competitiveness could further damage our political system.

The lessons on presidential and congressional elections emphasize the increasing costs of conducting political campaigns. Therefore, this lesson provides a foundation for understanding who pays for these ever more expensive campaigns.

There have been many suggestions for reforming the PAC system, including the idea of eliminating the need for PACS by financing congressional elections with public funds as we do the presidential elections. However, unless we the citizens pressure our elected officials to reform the system of political action committees in some way, Congress itself is not likely to "slap the hands that feed it."

Learning Objectives

Goal: The purpose of "The Power of PACs" is to create an awareness of why political action committees are created, how their contributions affect the federal electoral process, and the kind of support their money generates for PAC-related issues.

Objectives:

1. Explain how PAC funding for candidates works, in terms of the rules set by the 1974 Federal Election Campaign Act, suggested changes in campaign-finance laws, and potential abuses of PAC funds.

2. Describe the origin and evolution of political action committees, including why they exist, what they do, what they receive in return, and why they have grown so rapidly.

3. Compare the rationale for, and legal limitations on, individuals contributing to PACs rather than directly to candidates.

4. Outline Larry Sabato's arguments for and against PACs, and illustrate what effect PACs may have on our representative form of government.

5. Identify the type of candidates most likely to receive contributions from PACs, and tell how PAC support affects voter choice and interest in elections.

Key Terms

Watch for these terms and pay particular attention to what each one means, as you follow the textbook and telelesson.

Political action committees (TV)
"Soft" money (TV)

Textbook Reading Assignment

Schmidt, Shelley, and Bardes. *American Government and Politics Today,* 1993-94 edition. Chapter 8, "Interest Groups," pp. 239-265. [This is the same reading assignment as for Lesson 7; therefore, review it carefully and focus on pp. 240, 256-257.]

Textbook Focus Points

Before you read the textbook assignment, review the following points to help focus your thoughts. After you complete the assignment, write out your responses to reinforce what you have learned.

1. How is a PAC funded, and what restrictions did the 1974 Federal Election Campaign Act place on these funds?

2. Why do political action committees contribute to political campaigns?

Telelesson Interviewees

The following individuals share their expertise in the telelesson:

Mike Andrews–Democrat; U.S.Representative, Texas
John Murphy–Professor, Georgetown University Law School
Larry J. Sabato–Professor of Political Science, University of Virginia
Pamela Sederholm–Government Affairs Consultant
Philip Stern–Author; Co-Chair, Citizens Against PACs
Mike Synar–Democrat; U.S. Representative, Oklahoma
Lon Williams–Former Congressional Candidate

Telelesson Focus Points

Before viewing the telelesson, read over the following points to help focus your thoughts. After the presentation, write out your responses to help you remember these important points.

1. What is a political action committee, and why do interest groups and corporations form PACs?

2. What are the basic functions of PACs?

3. Why do individuals give to PACs rather than directly to a candidate?

4. What would you need to do to form a PAC?

5. What are Larry Sabato's arguments for and against PACs, and how does he believe PACs affect our representative form of government?

6. Why has the number of PACs grown so rapidly?

7. How do PACs raise money?

8. Who is most likely to receive the most contributions from PACs?

9. According to Pamela Sederholm, what determines the size of a contribution that a PAC gives to a candidate?

10. What does Pamela Sederholm say PACs can expect from officials, in return for PAC campaign contributions?

11. According to Philip Stern, why are PACs a threat to democracy?

12. What are some suggestions for changes in campaign-finance laws, and what are the chances of any change being made?

Recommended Reading

The following suggestions are not required unless your instructor assigns them. They are listed to let you know where you can find additional information on areas which interest you.

Gorman, Christine. "The Price of Power." *Time* 132 (October 31, 1988): pp. 44-45.

Hackett, George, and Eleanor Clift. "For Members Only." *Newsweek* 112 (November 14, 1988): pp.22-23.

Ross, Irwin. "Why PACs Spell Trouble." *Reader's Digest* 123 (July 1983): pp. 108-113.

Sabato, Larry J. *PAC Power: Inside the World of Political Action Committees*. New York: Norton, 1984.

Sheler, Jeffery, L. "Is Congress for Sale?" *U.S. News & World Report* 96 (May 28, 1984): pp. 47-51.

Stern, Philip M. *The Best Congress Money Can Buy*. New York: Pantheon Books, 1988.

Getting Involved

These activities are not required unless your instructor assigns them. But they offer good suggestions to help you understand and become more involved in the political process.

1. Contact your U.S. Representative or Senator. Ask if he or she accepts PAC contributions, and the reasons why or why not.

---

2. Contact Common Cause [2030 M Street N.W., Washington, D.C. 20036, phone: 202-833-1200]. Ask for information about Common Cause's arguments for and against PACs, and what campaign-finance reforms Common Cause supports.

Self Test

After reading the assignment and watching the telelesson, you should be able to answer these questions. When you have completed the test, turn to the Answer Key to score your answers.

1. The 1974 Federal Election Campaign Act and its 1976 amendments allow interest groups, corporations, and labor unions to raise money for candidates by
   a. holding fund-raising activities in congressional districts.
   b. borrowing from banks that support a particular candidate.
   c. collecting $1.00 from each federal income - tax return.
   d. setting up political action committees (PACs).

2. Interest groups use political action committee (PAC) contributions as a way to
   a. guarantee that legislators will vote for their proposals.
   b. increase access to powerful legislators.
   c. legally increase the pay of a specific member of Congress.
   d. disassociate themselves from campaign contributions.

3. An organization established by a labor union, interest group, or corporate employees for the purpose of raising and donating money to political candidates is called a
   a. labor movement.
   b. interest group.
   c. political action committee.
   d. service sector.

4. One of the basic functions of a PAC is to
   a. raise money from individuals and donate that money to candidates.
   b. act as a watchdog over the behavior of elected officials and reprimand them when they behave unethically.
   c. serve as treasurer for a candidate's election campaign and file the financial reports.
   d. research topics for the interest group and provide the information to elected officials.

5. Which of the following is NOT a reason for individuals to give to PACs instead of directly to a candidate?
   a. Individuals depend on PACs to evaluate the candidates and then donate to the best qualified.
   b. PACs pool individual donations and make one large donation to a candidate.
   c. Federal election laws limit the amount an individual can contribute.
   d. There is no limit to the total amount a PAC can contribute.

6. All that an interest group has to do to form a PAC is
   a. have 2,000 members of the interest group sign a petition to create a PAC.
   b. raise $50,000 to prove that it is a viable organization.
   c. register with the attorney general's office.
   d. register with the Federal Election Commission.

7. Larry Sabato argues in favor of PACs because they
   a. have a constitutional basis and are supported by numerous organizations.
   b. present a broad range of issues and encourage challengers to run against incumbents.
   c. reduce the opportunity for financial campaign abuse and allow more people to contribute.
   d. increase participation and provide money which is vital to the political process.

8. One reason for the increased number of PACs is the 1974 revision of federal campaign-finance laws which
   a. provided for the creation of interest groups.
   b. specified how campaign funds could be appropriated.
   c. prohibited interest groups from donating directly to a candidate.
   d. designated the total amount that candidates could spend on a campaign.

9. Political action committees receive the money they donate to candidates from
   a. individual contributions.
   b. corporate donations.
   c. fund-raising activities.
   d. labor-union contributions.

10. A major portion of PAC funds go to
    a. challengers.
    b. incumbents.
    c. political parties.
    d. lobbyists.

11. According to Pamela Sederholm, which of the following factors does NOT determine how much money a PAC will contribute to a candidate?
    a. The campaign laws
    b. The PAC budget
    c. The candidate's support of the PAC's objectives
    d. The candidate's political party

12. When a PAC makes a campaign contribution, Pamela Sederholm says it does NOT expect
    a. employment for its members.
    b. support for its issues.
    c. access to the candidate.
    d. political accountability.

13. Philip Stern believes that PACs are a threat to democracy because members of Congress become dependent on groups outside their congressional districts or states for their political money and because
    a. PACs are difficult to hold accountable.
    b. PACs contribute overwhelmingly to incumbents over challengers.
    c. elected officials are always busy getting re-elected.
    d. the issues are too complex for them to truly represent their constituents.

14. Philip Stern advocates such campaign-finance reforms as
    a. limiting the total amount that PACs can donate and requiring strict accounting of funds.
    b. making PACs contribute through the political parties and putting a ceiling on the amount that can be donated.
    c. eliminating all PAC donations to federal candidates and establishing public financing for congressional races.
    d. requiring a finance report from each campaign and using the Federal Election Commission to investigate irregularities.

Short-Answer Question:

15. What are some possible changes to the current methods of financing campaigns, and why do you think politicians would be for or against these proposals?

Answer Key

These are the correct answers with reference to the Learning Objectives, and to the source of the information: the Textbook Focus Points, Schmidt, *et al. American Government and Politics Today* (Schmidt), and the Telelesson Focus Points. Page numbers are also given for the Textbook Focus Points. "KT" indicates questions with Key Terms defined.

Question	Answer	Learning Objective	Textbook Focus Point (page no.)	Telelesson Focus Point
1	D	1	1 (Schmidt, p. 256)	KT
2	B	2	2 (Schmidt, p. 256)	
3	C	2		1
4	A	2		2
5	A	3		3
6	D	2		4
7	D	4		5
8	C	2		6
9	A	2		7
10	B	5		8
11	D	3		9
12	A	2		10
13	B	1		11
14	C	1		12

Short Answer:

15		1		12

Lesson 9

Government and the Media

Overview

Nearly every home in the United States has at least one television set, and most of us also listen to the radio and read a newspaper or newsmagazine. But who decides what news we can see on television or hear on the radio, and what will appear in print? The various mass media themselves! This lesson points out the effects of the news media on politics and describes how the media set the national political agenda or react to agenda policy.

The government and the media seem to form a mutual admiration society. One needs the other to successfully achieve its goals. The government uses a number of techniques to provide the mass media with information: off-the-record meetings, the presidential schedule, the timing of presidential news releases, the proverbial "tip," trial balloons, and the anonymous "leak." The members of the media who are most skillful at obtaining this information and building on it increase their number of readers, listeners, or viewers; enlarge their profits; and ultimately attain the power to set and control the political agenda.

In this lesson we view several examples of how the news media handled three specific situations: American hostages held in Iran, South African equal rights demonstrations, and the Manassas, Virginia, "Save the Battlefield" campaign. How the various media addressed each situation demonstrates the power of the media to either set an agenda or react to public policy.

This lesson also raises the question: Should Americans accept what the mass media present as a true reflection of society's problems and concerns? We as Americans must be aware of government and media manipulation, so that we can demand more credibility and accountability from each participant in the political-agenda game.

Learning Objectives

Goal: The purpose of "Government and the Media" is to spotlight the effects of mass media on politics and describe how the news media can set the public agenda or simply react to public policy.

Objectives:

1. Outline the roles of broadcast and print media in a democracy, tracing the changes from colonial days to the present.

2. Explain why television is the most influential of the media and how smart politicians use the media to their advantage.

3. Describe the power of the media, especially as it relates to campaigns for political office and decisions by public officials.

4. List methods used by the government to regulate and influence the media, and the effect this has on the political process.

5. Justify the need for the public to have access to news media, using the opinions of Stephanie Greco-Larson and Jeff Greenfield to support your argument.

6. Define the terms "agenda setting," "tips," and "trial balloons" as they relate to the role of the media in the political process.

7. Explain the reasons why the media react to events as opposed to setting an agenda, using supporting evidence from the Iranian hostage situation and Jimmy Carter's re-election effort, the South African equal rights demonstrations, and the Manassas Battlefield controversy.

Key Terms

Watch for these terms and pay particular attention to what each one means, as you follow the textbook and telelesson.

Managed news	**Media access**
Yellow journalism	**Agenda setting (TV)**
Electronic media	**Off-the-record meeting (TV)**
Paid-for political announcement	**Presidential schedule (TV)**
Spin	**Tip (TV)**
Public agenda	**Trial balloon (TV)**
	Leak (TV)

Textbook Reading Assignment

Schmidt, Shelley, and Bardes. *American Government and Politics Today,* 1993-94 edition. Chapter 11, "The Media," pp. 345-373.

Textbook Focus Points

Before you read the textbook assignment, review the following points to help focus your thoughts. After you complete the assignment, write out your responses to reinforce what you have learned.

1. What functions should mass media perform?

2. How has the role of mass media changed in the United States from colonial days to the present?

3. How have smart politicians used the electromagnetic signal of television?

4. Why is television the most influential of the media?

---

5. What kind of political power does television wield in campaigns for the presidency and other national offices?

6. How significant are televised presidential debates?

7. How do the media wield power over government and its officials?

8. What is the relationship between the media and the president?

9. How does government regulate the media?

10. Why should the public have access to the media?

Telelesson Interviewees

The following individuals share their expertise in the telelesson:

Mike Andrews–Democrat; U.S. Representative, Texas
Stephanie Greco-Larson–Professor of Political Science, The George Washington University, Washington, D.C.
Jeff Greenfield–Political and Media Analyst, ABC News
Ron Nessen–Former Press Secretary, President Ford's Administration
Jody Powell–Former Press Secretary, President Carter's Administration
Clint Schemmer–Former Manassas (Virginia) Bureau Chief, *Potomac News*
Annie Snyder–Co-chair, Committee to Save the Battlefield, Manassas, Virginia

Telelesson Focus Points

Before viewing the telelesson, read over the following points to help focus your thoughts. After the presentation, write out your responses to help you remember these important points.

1. What is "agenda setting," and what role do the mass media play in setting the agenda?

2. How did the news media's coverage of the Iranian hostage situation set an agenda, and what influence did this coverage have on Jimmy Carter's bid for re-election?

3. What effect did media coverage have on the South African equal rights demonstrations becoming part of the agenda in the United States?

4. How did the news media help the Manassas Battlefield controversy become a part of the national agenda?

5. What methods do government officials use to influence the media?

6. How do government officials use tips and trial balloons to affect the national agenda?

7. According to Stephanie Greco-Larson and Jeff Greenfield, to what extent are the media a true reflection of society's views and concerns?

Recommended Reading

The following suggestions are not required unless your instructor assigns them. They are listed to let you know where you can find additional information on areas which interest you.

Alter, Jonathan. "How the Media Blew It." *Newsweek* 112 (November 21, 1988): pp. 24-26.

Barnes, Fred. "Can We Trust the News?" *Reader's Digest* 132 (January 1988): pp. 33-38.

Graber, Doris T. *Media Power in Politics*. Washington, D.C.: Congressional Quarterly Press, 1984.

McLoughlin, M. "Television's Blinding Power." *U.S. News & World Report* 103 (July 27, 1987): pp. 18-21.

White, Theodore H. *The Making of the President, 1960*. New York: Atheneum Publishers, 1961.

Getting Involved

These activities are not required unless your instructor assigns them. But they offer good suggestions to help you understand and become more involved in the political process.

1. Note the "Getting Involved" section in your textbook at the end of Chapter 11.

2. Choose a day to watch two or three major network news programs, then compare the stories that each network covers–the similarities and the differences. Pay particular attention to how the various networks cover the same story.

Self Test

After reading the assignment and watching the telelesson, you should be able to answer these questions. When you have completed the test, turn to the Answer Key to score your answers.

1. A primary goal of the mass media, when they cover government and politics, is to
   a. influence the audience to adopt a particular point of view.
   b. indoctrinate the public.
   c. attract a larger audience.
   d. report the news.

2. The role of the media in the founding of the United States was
   a. of little or no importance.
   b. much more important than the media is today.
   c. no different than the role of the media in today's society.
   d. not as overwhelmingly important as the role of the media today.

3. Which of the following is NOT used by smart politicians to stay newsworthy?
   a. They attack the president's programs.
   b. They leak a story to the press to focus attention on their reaction.
   c. They hold highly visible hearings on controversial subjects.
   d. They go on "fact-finding" trips.

4. The most interesting aspect of television, that also has great influence on viewers, is the fact that it
   a. focuses on the truth rather than on sensationalism.
   b. features obscure facts rather than current issues.
   c. relies on pictures rather than words.
   d. takes the unpopular view rather than the most popular.

5. The reason candidates and their consultants spend much of their time devising strategies to use television to their benefit is because television
   a. is the primary news source for the majority of Americans.
   b. recruits campaign consultants to analyze the political scene.
   c. appeals to all ages and ethnic backgrounds.
   d. gives the most extensive coverage of all the candidates and issues.

6. With all the risks of debates, the potential for gaining votes is so great that candidates undoubtedly will
   a. avoid televised debates.
   b. continue to seek televised debates.
   c. find other ways to attract media attention.
   d. recruit media experts to perform for them.

7. Although studies have shown that the media may not have as much power to change people's minds as we thought, one of the media's greatest powers is their ability to
   a. report questionable behavior of elected officials in order to make public servants more accountable.
   b. focus attention on the international market and its effect on our trade deficit.
   c. shape the public agenda by focusing on public problems and specific political leaders.
   d. report the news without having to complete extensive research on the topic.

8. The relationship between the presidency and the news media has been
   a. testy.
   b. reciprocal.
   c. unethical.
   d. elusive.

9. Although the First Amendment states that Congress shall make no law abridging freedom of the press, the government regulates electronic media through the
   a. National Association of Broadcasters.
   b. Federal Communications Commission.
   c. Public Broadcasting Commission.
   d. Federal Association of Communications.

10. Americans have a right to access broadcast media because the
   a. people have a right to information from the media.
   b. government has the right to decide how public airways are used.
   c. government owns the airwaves and broadcast media.
   d. broadcast companies recognize their special responsibilities to the public.

11. By influencing the selection of policy alternatives and directing the focus of a political, economic, or social crisis, the media play a major role in
   a. agenda setting.
   b. electronic media.
   c. media access.
   d. White House corps.

12. When Americans were taken hostage in Iran, the American media did NOT
   a. appeal to the anger and outrage of the American people by plastering the TV screens with pictures of the hostages bound and blindfolded.
   b. create special network programs, such as "Nightline," to give the hostage crisis extra coverage.
   c. cover the humiliating attempt of President Carter to rescue the hostages.
   d. fill newspapers and magazines with pages on the story and add special sections to make room for extra coverage.

13. Which of the following was NOT a reason for the media's extensive coverage of South Africa's equal rights demonstrations?
    a. The pictures showed violent confrontations between demonstrators and government police.
    b. The television networks had a story that appealed to the public.
    c. The question of U.S. policy toward South Africa had become a national debate.
    d. The pictures of violent demonstrations revealed that other nations experience discrimination problems, too.

14. After an earlier visit to the Manassas Battlefield, Congressman Mike Andrews's attention was refocused on the battlefield when
    a. the developer lobbied Mike Andrews for a federal grant to build the shopping center.
    b. he read a newspaper article about the developer wanting to build a shopping center across from the battlefield.
    c. residents of Manassas appealed to Congress for a grant to purchase and restore the battlefield.
    d. a local television station interviewed the developer and restoration group.

15. Manipulation, a technique used by both media and government, is
    a. a reciprocal action.
    b. an illegal action.
    c. yellow journalism.
    d. an executive agreement.

16. The president battles the media for control of the nation's agenda by using such weapons as
    a. news conferences and leaks.
    b. trial balloons and the presidential schedule.
    c. tips and trial balloons.
    d. presidential news conferences and the presidential schedule.

Short-Answer Question:

17. After listening to Stephanie Greco-Larson and Jeff Greenfield, do you think Americans should accept what the media present to us as a true reflection of society's problems or concerns? Why or why not?

Answer Key

These are the correct answers with reference to the Learning Objectives, and to the source of the information: the Textbook Focus Points, Schmidt, *et al. American Government and Politics Today* (Schmidt), and the Telelesson Focus Points. Page numbers are also given for the Textbook Focus Points. "KT" indicates questions with Key Terms defined.

Question	Answer	Learning Objective	Textbook Focus Point (page no.)	Telelesson Focus Point
1	D	1	1 (Schmidt, p. 348)	
2	D	1	2 (Schmidt, p. 350)	
3	B	2	3 (Schmidt, p. 353)	
4	C	2	4 (Schmidt, p. 354)	
5	A	3	5 (Schmidt, p. 357)	
6	B	3	6 (Schmidt, p. 362)	
7	C	3	7 (Schmidt, p. 360) .... KT	
8	B	3	8 (Schmidt, p. 364)	
9	B	4	9 (Schmidt, p. 366).......... KT	
10	B	5	10 (Schmidt, p. 370)	
11	A	6	KT	1
12	C	7		2
13	D	7		3
14	B	7		4
15	A	4		5
16	C	6	KT	6

Short Answer:

17		5		7

Lesson 10

Political Parties

Overview

Political parties may seem far removed, but they are actually you, I, and our neighbors—the "grass roots"—who want to participate in the political system, beginning at the local level and progressing to the state and national levels. The "grass roots" participants form the backbone of political parties.

This is important because political parties perform a vital function in the United States political system: They are the avenues by which we select candidates and elect officials to govern us.

In an attempt to appeal to more people and to justify their existence, in the 1970s and 1980s both major parties broadened their membership and democratized their methods for selecting presidential candidates. But, in doing this, each party weakened its power to act with one voice.

No doubt you frequently are asked if you are a Democrat or a Republican; sometimes you are even asked why. In this lesson we address the similarities and differences between the two major parties and review the philosophies of each. We also investigate the need for political parties: What they are, what they do, and how they began. In the process we take a closer look at the two-party system itself, especially its characteristics and functions.

The point of this lesson is to help you better understand the political system in the United States—and the part you can play in affecting the direction in which it goes.

Learning Objectives

Goal: The purpose of "Political Parties" is to explain why the United States has only two major political parties and illustrate how the two parties influence individual political participation.

Objectives:

1. Describe political parties–what they are, what their functions and goals are, how they are structured, and why people join them.

2. Trace the evolution of political parties, emphasizing their impact on government in the United States from the time of the Constitutional Convention to the present.

3. List factors which promoted growth of the two-party system in the United States, and discuss the role of third parties in a two-party system.

4. Contrast the philosophies of the Democratic and Republican parties, including the positives and negatives of recent party reforms.

5. Outline the strengths and weaknesses of political parties, and describe movements for renewal and reform.

6. Explain the effects of the winner-take-all system of electing candidates on the membership and on the issues of a political party.

7. Show how the "grass roots" level, the rank-and-file members, affect a political party.

Key Terms

Watch for these terms and pay particular attention to what each one means, as you follow the textbook and telelesson.

Political party	Patronage
Faction	Two-party system
Two-party competition	Plurality system
Party-in-government	Third party
National convention	Party identification
Party platform	Ticket splitting
National committee	Independent voter
Unit rule	Grass roots(TV)

Textbook Reading Assignment

Schmidt, Shelley, and Bardes. *American Government and Politics Today*, 1993-94 edition. Chapter 9, "Political Parties," pp. 267-297.

Textbook Focus Points

Before you read the textbook assignment, review the following points to help focus your thoughts. After you complete the assignment, write out your responses to reinforce what you have learned.

1. What are political parties?

2. What are the functions of political parties in the United States?

3. How have political parties evolved in the United States, and what impact have they had on government?

4. How are political parties structured, in theory and in action?

5. Why do we have a two-party system in the United States?

6. How do the Democratic and Republican parties differ today?

7. What role have minor, or third, parties played in U.S. political history?

8. Are political parties in the United States a thing of the past?

Telelesson Interviewees

The following individuals share their expertise in the telelesson:

Lee Atwater–Former Chair, Republican National Committee
David Broder–Journalist, *The Washington Post*
Ron Brown–Former Chair, Democratic National Committee
Everret Carll Ladd–Director, Roper Center for Public Opinion and
    Research; Professor, University of Connecticut
Fred Myer–Chair, Republican Party of Texas
Deborah Wood–Volunteer, Democratic Party

Telelesson Focus Points

Before viewing the telelesson, read over the following points to help focus your thoughts. After the presentation, write out your responses to help you remember these important points.

1. What is the primary goal of a political party, and how does it attain its goal?

2. What are the major differences between the Democratic and Republican parties and between their recent platforms?

3. How has the winner-take-all system affected the membership and the issues of the political parties?

4. What role do the "grass roots" play in political parties?

5. What problems have party reforms created for the political parties?

6. What do you believe the future holds for the Democratic and Republican parties?

Recommended Reading

The following suggestions are not required unless your instructor assigns them. They are listed to let you know where you can find additional information on areas which interest you.

Gergen, David R. "America's Split Personality Government: Why Voters Won't Give One Party the White House and the Congress." *U.S. News & World Report* 105 (November 21, 1988): pp. 36-38.

Gitelson, Alan R., M. Margaret Conway, and Frank B. Feigert. *American Political Parties: Stability and Change.* Boston: Houghton Mifflin, 1984.

Sabato, Larry J. *The Party Has Just Begun: Shaping Political Parties for America's Future.* Boston: Scott Foresman, 1988.

Getting Involved

These activities are not required unless your instructor assigns them. But they offer good suggestions to help you understand and become more involved in the political process.

1. Visit the county headquarters of the political party of your choice to learn how the party is organized, what it does, and what you can do to help.

2. Many communities have informal local political-party organizations. Locate one of your choice, visit some of its meetings or social events, and decide if you would like to participate further in its activities.

3. Note the "Getting Involved" section in your textbook at the end of Chapter 9. Follow the suggestions and be ready to participate in your next state and national elections.

Self Test

After reading the assignment and watching the telelesson, you should be able to answer these questions. When you have completed the test, turn to the Answer Key to score your answers.

1. A political party is a group of individuals who have
   a. agreed on all policy issues.
   b. some measure of policy agreement.
   c. paid monthly dues to an ideological organization.
   d. been elected to office and obtained a position of power.

2. Which of the following is NOT a function of political parties in the United States?
   a. Recruiting candidates for public office
   b. Organizing and running elections
   c. Presenting alternative policies to the electorate
   d. Developing a national economic policy

3. The goal of American political parties is
   a. signing up large numbers of deeply committed members.
   b. winning elections and gaining party majorities in Congress.
   c. collecting dues from members to support candidates.
   d. developing ideas that are ideologically correct for the party.

4. A major impact of early political parties on government was the
   a. need to control campaign contributions.
   b. peaceful transfer of power from one group to another.
   c. decrease in voter turnout in the United States.
   d. increase in corrupt political transactions.

5. In reality, the formal structure of American political parties resembles
   a. a pyramid-shaped organization.
   b. a layer cake with autonomous levels.
   c. an English model of representative democracy.
   d. an inverted pyramid-shaped organization.

6. In general, a strong national chairperson has considerable power over
   a. party members in Congress.
   b. writers of the party platform.
   c. advisors of the candidates for office.
   d. state-level members.

7. A major part of the historical basis for a two-party system in the United States was the development of
   a. interests split along geographic lines.
   b. British political philosophy.
   c. parties in colonial legislatures.
   d. ethnic-group participation in the early 1800s.

8. In general, the Democratic party has NOT received much support from
   a. Jewish voters.
   b. union voters.
   c. professionals.
   d. women.

9. The most successful minor, or third, parties have
   a. stressed far-right ideological issues.
   b. restrained the power of parties in Congress.
   c. spun off from major parties.
   d. based their platforms on religious beliefs.

10. Which one of the following reasons has NOT weakened party ties?
    a. Dramatic increase in minority population
    b. Increased importance of media in American politics
    c. Higher educational levels of Americans
    d. The mobility of American voters

11. The primary goal of a political party is to
    a. recruit better qualified candidates to run for office.
    b. raise enough funds to finance most national campaigns.
    c. enroll new members to fill the volunteer positions.
    d. gain political power by winning a majority of elective offices.

12. Recent Democratic and Republican platforms show that two major issues on which they disagree are
    a. commerce and mass transportation.
    b. space exploration and trade.
    c. military spending and balancing the budget.
    d. inflation and recession.

13. The winner-take-all system forces the two major parties to allow a
    a. limited combination of issues and people.
    b. diverse mix of ideas and people.
    c. narrow diversity of member interests.
    d. membership dedicated only to party goals.

14. Which of the following is NOT supplied by "grass roots" activists?
    a. Future leaders
    b. Dedicated, motivated volunteers
    c. Citizen input
    d. Large financial resources

15. What was NOT accomplished by the political-party reforms of the 1970s and 1980s?
    a. Reforms allowed "grass roots" citizens to have a voice in selecting candidates for public office.
    b. Reforms prevented party members from voting for a Republican presidential candidate and a Democratic congressional candidate.
    c. Reforms encouraged women and minorities to participate in the political system.
    d. Reforms reduced the power of the national party leaders.

Short-Answer Question:

16. What do you believe the future holds for the Democratic and Republican parties?

Answer Key

These are the correct answers with reference to the Learning Objectives, and to the source of the information: the Textbook Focus Points, Schmidt, *et al. American Government and Politics Today* (Schmidt), and the Telelesson Focus Points. Page numbers are also given for the Textbook Focus Points. "KT" indicates questions with Key Terms defined.

Question	Answer	Learning Objective	Textbook Focus Point (page no.)	Telelesson Focus Point
1	B	1	1 (Schmidt, p. 269)............KT	
2	D	1	2 (Schmidt, pp. 269-270)	
3	B	1	2 (Schmidt, p. 271)	1
4	B	2	3 (Schmidt, p. 272)	
5	B	1	4 (Schmidt, p. 277)	
6	D	1	4 (Schmidt, p. 280)	
7	A	3	5 (Schmidt, p. 288)............KT	
8	C	4	6 (Schmidt, p. 289)	
9	C	3	7 (Schmidt, p. 292)............KT	
10	A	5	8 (Schmidt, p. 295)	
11	D	1	KT	1
12	C	4		2
13	B	6		3
14	D	7	KT	4
15	B	5		5

Short Answer:

16		5		6

Lesson 11

Nominating a President

Overview

Nominating a president of the United States is an important and exciting part of the American political process. The official nominating process by the two major political parties occurs once every four years. It lasts approximately six to seven months and culminates at their national conventions. Unofficially, candidates who seek the presidential nomination may begin the process years earlier.

This lesson addresses the reasons why a candidate would seek the presidential nomination, then examines the long, arduous, and expensive road to the nomination. It describes how state parties select their delegates to the national conventions and relates some of the activities that lead to the ultimate reason for a convention: nominating a candidate for president and one for vice president to run in the November general election.

The national conventions also serve as big pep rallies for the political parties to focus national attention on their candidates and to increase support and energy for the final phase in the quest for the presidency.

The nominating process has become more democratic just since the 1960s, because of the reforms that have taken place in both major political parties. Primaries are more prevalent, delegates are more representative of the general citizenry, and federal laws try to regulate campaigns to make them more equitable for all candidates. Changes continue to occur, such as the March 1988 Super Tuesday, and the suggested national presidential primary might be next.

The nominating process is not the final step in selecting a president. But it offers you a voice in deciding who one of the choices will be in the November general election.

Learning Objectives

Goal: The purpose of "Nominating a President" is to describe the presidential nominating process in the United States and to explain how recent changes allow greater individual participation.

Objectives:

1. Describe qualifications required for becoming a presidential candidate and the decisions an individual must make before deciding to pursue the presidency.

2. Illustrate the campaign trail leading to a national nominating convention, by contrasting the nomination process prior to 1965 with that of today.

3. Explain the strategy for developing a winning campaign for the presidential nomination, including fundraising, the role of television, and opportunities for citizen involvement.

4. Contrast arguments for and against a national presidential primary, in the context of proposed and adopted reforms in both the primary system and the March 1988 Super Tuesday.

5. Assess the useful functions and different types of party caucuses, state conventions and presidential primaries—including the Iowa caucus and the New Hampshire primary—as methods by which political parties within a state select national convention delegates.

6. Describe the convention method of nominating presidential candidates, including the increased role of media, decreased roles of parties and conventions, and differences in how states select their convention delegates.

Key Terms

Watch for these terms and pay particular attention to what each one means, as you follow the textbook and telelesson.

Political consultant
Image building
Independent candidate
Federal Election Commission
Presidential primary
Caucus
Closed primary

Open primary
Blanket primary
Run-off primary
1974 Campaign Reform Act (TV)
Proportional primary (TV)
Super Tuesday (TV)

Textbook Reading Assignment

Schmidt, Shelley, and Bardes. *American Government and Politics Today*, 1993-94 edition. Chapter 10, "Campaigns, Candidates, and Elections," pp. 299-320.

Textbook Focus Points

Before you read the textbook assignment, review the following points to help focus your thoughts. After you complete the assignment, write out your responses to reinforce what you have learned.

1. Why would an individual run for political office?

2. What are the constitutional requirements for individuals seeking the office of president or vice president?

3. How has the presidential nominating campaign changed?

4. What considerations go into developing a strategy for winning the presidential nomination?

5. How do candidates for the presidential nomination raise funds, and what restrictions have been placed on fundraising?

6. How has the primary system been reformed?

7. What useful functions do the presidential primaries serve?

8. What different types of primaries are held today?

9. What are the arguments for and against a national presidential primary?

10. How does the convention method of nominating presidential candidates work?

Telelesson Interviewees

The following individuals share their expertise in the telelesson:

Lee Atwater–Former Chair, Republican National Committee; Manager, George Bush's 1988 Presidential Campaign
Jeff Greenfield–Political and Media Analyst, ABC News
Andrea Mitchell–Chief Congressional Correspondent, NBC News

Telelesson Focus Points

Before viewing the telelesson, read over the following points to help focus your thoughts. After the presentation, write out your responses to help you remember these important points.

1. How were nominees for president chosen prior to 1968? How has this changed today?

2. How do states select delegates to the national convention?

3. Why are the Iowa caucus and the New Hampshire primary so important to presidential candidates?

4. What was the purpose of the March 1988 Super Tuesday primary?

5. What role does television play in nominating a president?

Recommended Reading

The following suggestions are not required unless your instructor assigns them. They are listed to let you know where you can find additional information on areas which interest you.

Davis, James. *Presidential Primaries.* New York: Greenwood Press, 1984.

Diamond, Edwin. "The New Rules of the Game." *New Yorker* 21, no. 2 (January 11, 1988): p. 8+.

Polsby, Nelson W., and Aaron Wildavsky. "The Nominating Process" in *Presidential Elections*, 6th edition, New York: Charles Scribner's Sons, 1984.

Reiter, Howard L."Presidential Elections" in *Parties and Elections in Corporate America*. New York: St. Martin's Press, 1987.

Shapiro, W. "A Bartered Nomination?" *Time* 131 (February 29, 1988): pp. 42-43.

Wayne, Steven J. *The Road to the White House: The Politics of Presidential Elections*, 3rd edition. New York: St. Martin Press, 1988.

Getting Involved

These activities are not required unless your instructor assigns them. But they offer good suggestions to help you understand and become more involved in the political process.

1. You will be unable to vote in the primaries, and thus have no voice in the nomination process, unless you are registered to vote. Refer to the "Getting Involved" section at the end of Chapter 10 and register to vote, so that you can cast your ballot in upcoming elections.

2. Select a candidate for the next presidential nomination, locate the candidate's closest campaign office, and volunteer to work in the campaign. (If no presidential election will be held soon, volunteer to help in your next local, county, state, or referendum election. This will give you political-campaign experience and contacts, preparing you to work even more effectively in the next presidential campaign.)

Self Test

After reading the assignment and watching the telelesson, you should be able to answer these questions. When you have completed the test, turn to the Answer Key to score your answers.

1. People choose to run for political office because they
   a. want to further their political careers or respond to certain issues.
   b. are leaders of interest groups and want recognition.
   c. want to make money and seek financial contacts.
   d. like people or want to leave something for posterity.

2. Which of the following is NOT a constitutional requirement for a candidate seeking the office of President?
   a. Must be a natural-born citizen
   b. Must have attained the age of 35 years
   c. Must be a resident of the country for 14 years by the time of the inauguration
   d. Must have held an elective office

3. What has happened to campaigns in the last decade reflects the
   a. change from party-centered campaigning to candidate-centered campaigning.
   b. increased importance of campaigning on a personal basis and less emphasis on the media.
   c. major increase in money that candidates receive from their party.
   d. lack of attention paid to the results of public opinion polls.

4. To run a successful campaign, the candidate's organization must
   a. refrain from entering into a policy debate with the organizations of the other candidates.
   b. convince the national party to back the financial cost of the campaign.
   c. use as much deception as possible without violating the law.
   d. be able to raise funds for the campaign.

5. The Federal Election Campaign Act of 1974 provided
   a. money for candidates to borrow at a lower interest rate than the current market value.
   b. public financing for presidential primaries and presidential candidates in the general election.
   c. a $1 million payment to candidates seeking a party's nomination.
   d. that campaign contributions cannot exceed $100 to any one candidate.

6. Nominating presidential candidates is influenced by the
   a. party rank and file, rather than by party elites.
   b. members of the party in Congress.
   c. members of the electoral college.
   d. national party chairperson and the national executive committee.

7. The presidential primary performs several useful functions, such as
   a. allowing the media to cover the inside strategies of all the candidates and to interview each one personally.
   b. giving the party elites an opportunity to speak out and the candidates a forum in which to respond.
   c. presenting the candidates with fund-raising contacts and the means by which to collect the funds.
   d. providing an opportunity for the candidates to organize their campaigns and to try out different policy positions on the public.

8. The two most common types of primaries are the
   a. open primary and the run-off primary.
   b. blanket primary and the run-off primary.
   c. open primary and the closed primary.
   d. Closed primary and the blanket primary.

9. One argument against a national presidential primary is that it would
   a. deny independents the opportunity to select a candidate and to vote.
   b. be difficult for candidates to gain support unless they are well-known by the general public.
   c. eliminate the need for the electoral college and thus defeat the founders' purpose.
   d. place too much power in political parties for choosing the candidates.

10. The goal of any presidential hopeful at the national convention is to
    a. have media cover the family's arrival at the convention.
    b. meet as many delegates as possible before the convention convenes.
    c. obtain a majority of votes on the earliest ballot.
    d. give the Keynote Address on opening night.

11. Prior to 1968, the selection of presidential nominees was largely influenced by the
    a. speaker of the House and the Senate majority leader.
    b. outgoing president and party chairperson.
    c. party bosses.
    d. chief justice of the Supreme Court and speaker of the House.

12. Most state delegates to the national convention are selected by
    a. the state committee and state chairperson.
    b. the state legislature and governor.
    c. either a caucus or a primary election.
    d. a general election in the electoral college.

13. The Iowa caucus and the New Hampshire primary are important because they give candidates
    a. momentum and make it easier to raise money.
    b. the opportunity to determine if their tracking polls are accurate.
    c. an opportunity to evaluate how the media will ask their questions.
    d. a chance to screen their opponents and evaluate campaign strategy.

14. Which of the following was NOT a purpose of Super Tuesday?
    a. Combatting the influence of Iowa and New Hampshire on the presidential selection process
    b. Having the candidates address southern interests and needs
    c. Encouraging the South to vote as a bloc and influence who was nominated
    d. Showing the nation which candidate the South would support

15. Which one of the following has television NOT done?
    a. Replaced the party boss as the real power broker
    b. Determined a candidate's fate by deciding who is the front runner
    c. Provided free advertising to favored candidates
    d. Influenced the nomination by focusing on only one candidate

Short-Answer Question:

16. The telelesson asks the question, "Is this any way to nominate a president?" Do you think the current method is the best way? Why or why not? What suggestions can you make for reform?

Answer Key

These are the correct answers with reference to the Learning Objectives, Text Focus Points, and Telelesson Focus Points. Page numbers are also given for the Text Focus Points.

Question	Answer	Learning Objective	Text Focus Point (page no.)	Telelesson Focus Point
1	A	1	1 (p. 301)	1
2	D	1	2 (p. 303)	
3	A	2	3 (p. 305)	
4	D	3	4 (p. 305)	
5	B	3	5 (p. 314)	
6	A	4	6 (p. 315)	
7	D	5	7 (p. 316)	
8	C	5	8 (p. 317)	
9	B	4	9 (p. 319)	
10	C	6	10 (p. 320)	
11	C	2	3 (pp. 315-316)	1
12	C	5	6 (p. 316)	2
13	A	5		3
14	D	4		4
15	C	3		5

Short Answer:

16		6		1

Lesson 12

Presidential Campaigning

Overview

This lesson, "Presidential Campaigning," continues tracing the road to the White House. It takes us from the point at which a person is nominated by one of the major political parties until the winner takes the presidential oath of office.

In the process it identifies one of the misconceptions about electing a president: We never vote directly for the president or the vice president! So the lesson also addresses the various methods of selecting the people we actually do vote for: the electors who comprise the electoral college.

A previous lesson described the presidential nominating process: the strategies and components of seeking the nomination. Now we delve deeper into campaign strategy and how the existence of the electoral college affects the development of this strategy. We also identify other components of a campaign—including fund raising, polling, scheduling, and paid consultants—and the roles these play in shaping campaign strategy. The influence of the media is evident throughout.

Fewer than 5 percent of U.S citizens participate in presidential campaigns. Most individual influence is passive until election day; even then, less than 60 percent of the electorate votes. Suggested reforms in the campaign and the electoral college reflect attempts to increase individual participation.

All presidential campaigns are exciting and important, because we are electing one American citizen to what is acknowledged to be the most powerful public office in the world. Every means of traveling that long road to the White House still is fueled by those individuals who vote and who volunteer their time and skills in a presidential campaign.

Learning Objectives

Goal: The purpose of "Presidential Campaigning" is to illustrate factors that influence presidential campaigns, to describe the importance of the electoral college, and to show how individuals involved in the election affect the outcome.

Objectives:

1. State the characteristics of the electoral college, illustrating how the president and vice president are elected by it.

2. Explain the method for determining each state's number of electors in the electoral college and how these electors determine who the next president will be, including what happens when no candidate receives a majority of the electoral vote.

3. Describe criticisms and proposed reforms of the electoral college, as well as of the entire presidential campaigning process.

4. List ways that individuals participate in and influence the presidential election process.

5. Explain how the existence of the electoral college affects the strategy of a presidential campaign.

6. Describe the effects of candidate image, polling, "soft money," and the media on shaping the strategy of a presidential campaign.

Key Terms

Watch for these terms and pay particular attention to what each one means, as you follow the textbook and telelesson.

Elector
Electoral college
Plurality
Unit basis (winner takes all)

Polling (TV)
Soft money (TV)
Fund raising (TV)

Textbook Reading Assignment

Schmidt, Shelley, and Bardes. *American Government and Politics Today,* 1993-94 edition. Chapter 10, "Campaigns, Candidates, and Elections," pp. 320-323. [The remainder of the chapter is not covered in this lesson, but pp. 323-333 will give you a fuller understanding of the election process.]

Textbook Focus Points

Before you read the textbook assignment, review the following points to help focus your thoughts. After you complete the assignment, write out your responses to reinforce what you have learned.

1. What is the electoral college, and how are the president and vice president elected by it?

2. How is each state's number of electors determined?

3. If a candidate does not receive a majority of the electoral vote, who decides whom the next president and vice president will be and how does this work?

4. What are the major criticisms of the electoral college?

5. What are some reforms proposed for the electoral college?

Telelesson Interviewees

The following individuals share their expertise in the telelesson:

Lee Atwater–Former Chair, Republican National Committee; Manager, George Bush's 1988 Presidential Campaign

Susan Estrich–Manager, Michael Dukakis's 1988 Presidential Campaign

Susan Manes–Executive Vice President for Issue Development, Common Cause

George McGovern–Former U.S. Senator from South Dakota; 1972 Democratic Presidential Candidate

Telelesson Focus Points

Before viewing the telelesson, read over the following points to help focus your thoughts. After the presentation, write out your responses to help you remember these important points.

1. How do individuals participate in the presidential election process?

2. How does the existence of the electoral college shape the course and strategy of a presidential campaign?

3. How is the information that is gathered from polls used in a presidential campaign?

4. What is "soft money," and how is it used in a presidential campaign?

5. How does a candidate's image affect campaign strategy?

6. How are the various media used in presidential campaigning?

7. What reforms have been suggested for changing the way we elect a president?

Recommended Reading

The following suggestions are not required unless your instructor assigns them. They are listed to let you know where you can find additional information on areas which interest you.

Boller, Paul F. *Presidential Campaigns*. New York: Oxford University Press, 1984.

Forbes, M.S. "The Process Works." *Forbes* 141 (April 4, 1988): p. 25.

Polsby, Nelson W., and Aaron Wildavsky. "The Campaign" in *Presidential Elections*, 6th edition. New York: Charles Scribner's Sons, 1984.

Range, P.R. "The Lessons of Campaign '88." *U.S. News & World Report* 105 (November 7, 1988): pp. 18-19.

Wayne, Stephen. *The Road to the White House: The Politics of Presidential Elections*, 3rd edition. New York: St. Martin Press, 1988.

Getting Involved

These activities are not required unless your instructor assigns them. But they offer good suggestions to help you understand and become more involved in the political process.

1. Research and write a report about the most recent presidential election. Who were the candidates? What issues were emphasized? What gaffes were committed? Were there any minor-party candidates who affected the strategy of the major-party candidates? Did you vote? For which candidate? Why did you support that candidate? What changes would you recommend for the next election?

2. Contact the major political parties in your state. Find out who were on the slate of electors for each candidate in the last presidential election and how they were selected. Also ask the winning party in your state if any of its electors were "faithless."

Self Test

After reading the assignment and watching the telelesson, you should be able to answer these questions. When you have completed the test, turn to the Answer Key to score your answers.

1. The electoral college is
   a. a board composed of college presidents who advise presidential candidates.
   b. composed of individuals who think they might want to run for president in the next election.
   c. the group that actually elects the president and vice president.
   d. a committee of former presidents and vice presidents who advise presidential candidates.

2. The Constitution indicates that the number of presidential electors
   a. cannot exceed 550.
   b. cannot be changed without an amendment to the U.S. Constitution.
   c. is determined by the president every ten years after the census report.
   d. is equal to the number of U.S. Representatives and Senators plus three for the District of Columbia.

3. In cases where no presidential candidate receives a majority of the electoral college vote, the
   a. current president serves two more years, at which time another general election is held.
   b. candidate who receives a plurality of the popular vote is elected.
   c. electors cast a second vote to determine who will be elected.
   d. election is decided in the U.S. House of Representatives.

4. The founders' intent to have electors use their discretion has been negated, because the
   a. electors are exposed to media campaign rhetoric.
   b. electors do not have time to spend analyzing the qualities of the candidates.
   c. electors are legally committed to the candidate on whose slate they run.
   d. founders didn't allow for political parties nominating electors.

5. Which of the following proposals for reform of the electoral system has NOT been discussed?
   a. Abolishing the electoral college completely
   b. Requiring each elector to vote for the candidate who has a plurality in the state
   c. Letting the Senate choose a member for president and the House select the vice president
   d. Eliminating the electors but retaining the electoral vote

6. In which one of the following ways may individuals NOT participate in presidential elections?
   a. Voting in the general election
   b. Volunteering to work in a campaign
   c. Serving as a presidential elector
   d. Being a member of the U.S. Supreme Court

7. The most important problem that each presidential candidate faces is
   a. selecting a campaign manager who has political savvy.
   b. developing a strategy that will win a majority of the electoral college votes.
   c. deciding which television network to use for the majority of the campaign's press releases, in order to receive the most coverage.
   d. deciding on which coast to begin actively campaigning.

8. To which question do typical polls NOT seek an answer?
    a. Which candidate will you support?
    b. What is your stand on a particular issue?
    c. Which candidate's views on an issue most closely agree with your own?
    d. How much will you contribute to your candidate's campaign?

9. "Soft money" is money
    a. used in a campaign to purchase software for election research.
    b. donated by an industry from the candidate's home state.
    c. from women's groups directed to women's and children's issues.
    d. from corporate contributors funneled through state political parties.

10. Television is more personal than radio and has made
    a. image more important than issues.
    b. issues more important than image.
    c. candidates more careful about fund raising.
    d. candidates more attentive to issues.

11. Which one of the following will a campaign staff NOT do to improve name identification and recognition?
    a. Call a press conference for the candidate to make a special announcement regarding the campaign
    b. Produce a brief television spot extolling the candidate's virtues and personal accomplishments
    c. Produce a brief television spot directing attention to the opponent's weak characteristics or mistakes
    d. Announce who will serve in the cabinet if the candidate is elected

12. There have been several calls to change the way we elect a president; the most serious suggestion is to
    a. reduce the influence of Iowa and New Hampshire.
    b. allow Congress to screen candidates.
    c. strengthen the 1974 Campaign Reform Act.
    d. shorten the length of the campaign.

Short-Answer Question:

13. If you could make the choice as to how we elect a president, would you prefer the current method of the electoral college or a direct popular-vote election? Why?

Answer Key

These are the correct answers with reference to the Learning Objectives, and to the source of the information: the Textbook Focus Points, Schmidt, *et al. American Government and Politics Today* (Schmidt), and the Telelesson Focus Points. Page numbers are also given for the Textbook Focus Points. "KT" indicates questions with Key Terms defined.

Question	Answer	Learning Objective	Textbook Focus Point (page no.)		Telelesson Focus Point
1	C	1	1 (Schmidt, p. 320)	KT	2
2	D	2	2 (Schmidt, p. 322)	KT	1
3	D	2	3 (Schmidt, p. 322)	KT	
4	C	3	4 (Schmidt, p. 322)	KT	
5	C	3	5 (Schmidt, p. 323)		
6	D	4			1
7	B	5	1 (Schmidt, p. 322-323)		2
8	D	6			3
9	D	6		KT	4
10	A	6			5
11	D	6			6
12	D	3			7

Short Answer:

13		3	5 (Schmidt, pp. 322-323)	7

Lesson 13

Congressional Elections

Overview

Before deciding to seek a seat in the U.S. Senate or House of Representatives, individuals must answer many personal questions. They also must determine if they have a chance to win: Is there an incumbent? How strong is my base of support? How will I finance a campaign? Will I accept PAC contributions, rely on my personal wealth, or apply for personal loans? How might possible redistricting and reapportionment, as a result of the census, dilute my support or mean I suddenly have to face a more formidable opponent?

This lesson examines elections to the Congress of the United States. It surveys campaigns of candidates running for the first time and the re-election campaigns of incumbents.

It is one of a series dealing with elections: nominating a president, electing a president, and selecting U.S. senators and representatives. Elements from other lessons on interest groups, PACs, and political parties help you see how each component interacts within the political process and within the structure of government itself.

Those of us who choose not to become candidates still play two important roles in congressional elections. One, the backbone of most campaigns is the volunteers who carry out the campaign strategies designed by the professionals. Two, each of us needs to be well-informed about the candidates for congressional office and about the election process, so that we can cast our votes wisely.

Learning Objectives

Goal: The purpose of "Congressional Elections" is to contrast similarities and differences between running for the House of Representatives and the Senate in the United States and to illustrate factors which influence each race.

Objectives:

1. Describe the constitutional requirements and personal considerations that determine whether a person can run for the Senate or the House of Representatives.

2. Explain how the number of representatives and senators from each state is determined and how often each is elected.

3. Explain how midterm congressional elections and redistricting of House seats affect the party controlling the White House.

4. Outline the advantages of being an incumbent, including the significance of a "safe seat" and the major strategies members of Congress use to pursue re-election.

5. Describe campaign reforms that have occurred and those still needed in congressional elections, as well as how "equal protection of the laws" impacts state legislatures and congressional districts.

6. Illustrate the intricacies of a congressional campaign, including funding, television, direct mail, polling, political consultants, and use of volunteers.

7. Detail factors that influence Senate and House campaigns, and tell what it would take to get you to participate actively in a congressional campaign.

Key Terms

Watch for these terms and pay particular attention to what each one means, as you follow the textbook and telelesson.

Direct primaries
Midterm congressional elections
Reapportionment
Presentational style

Redistricting
Gerrymandering
Scheduling (TV)
Polling (TV)

Textbook Reading Assignment

Schmidt, Shelley, and Bardes. *American Government and Politics Today*, 1993-94 edition. Chapter 12, "The Congress," pp. 390-398. Also, reread Chapter 10, "Campaigns, Candidates, and Elections," pp. 299-315.

Textbook Focus Points

Before you read the textbook assignment, review the following points to help focus your thoughts. After you complete the assignment, write out your responses to reinforce what you have learned.

1. What are the constitutional requirements for a person running for the House or the Senate?

2. How is the number of representatives and senators from each state determined, and how often are each elected?

3. What are three major factors in determining who will run for congressional office?

4. What effect do midterm congressional elections have on the party controlling the White House?

5. What advantages does an incumbent have over a challenger?

---

6. What is the significance of a "safe seat" in a person's decision whether to run for Congress?

7. In what three major ways do members of Congress pursue re-election?

8. What impact does "equal protection of the laws" have on state legislatures and congressional districts?

9. What effect does redistricting have on House elections?

Telelesson Interviewees

The following individuals share their expertise in the telelesson:

John Bryant–Democrat; U.S. Representative, Texas
Elizabeth Drew–Journalist
Lisa LeMaster–Political Consultant; President, Fairchild LeMaster
Joseph Lieberman–Democrat; U.S. Senator, Connecticut
John Pouland–1988 Campaign Manager for Rep. John Bryant
Mike Synar–Democrat; U.S. Representative, Oklahoma
Lon Williams–Former Congressional Candidate

Telelesson Focus Points

Before viewing the telelesson, read over the following points to help focus your thoughts. After the presentation, write out your responses to help you remember these important points.

1. What factors influence a person's decision to run for the House or the Senate?

2. What are the advantages of being an incumbent?

3. What are the primary financial sources for a congressional candidate?

4. How is television used in a congressional campaign?

5. How is direct mail used in a congressional campaign?

6. How is polling used in a congressional campaign?

7. How are political consultants used in a congressional campaign?

8. How are volunteers used in a congressional campaign?

9. What reforms have occurred, and what ones are still needed, in congressional campaigns?

Recommended Reading

The following suggestions are not required unless your instructor assigns them. They are listed to let you know where you can find additional information on areas which interest you.

Evans, Rowland, and Robert Novak. "Congressmen for Life: The Incumbency Scandal." *Reader's Digest* (June 1989): pp. 79-83.

Henckley, Barbara. *Congressional Elections*. Washington, D.C.: Congressional Quarterly Press, 1981.

Howard, E. "Stacking the Deck: Advantages of Incumbent in Pennsylvania Congressional Race." *Common Cause Magazine* 15 (Jan./Feb. 1989):
pp. 24-26.

Reiter, Howard L. "Parties in Congress" in *Parties and Elections in Corporate America*. New York: St. Martin's Press, 1987.

Getting Involved

These activities are not required unless your instructor assigns them. But they offer good suggestions to help you understand and become more involved in the political process.

1. Congressional elections are held in even numbered years. If a congressional campaign is currently underway, become involved by contacting a candidate (incumbent or challenger) and volunteering to work in a campaign.

2. Contact your local member of Congress (or senator, if you live near the senator's office) and make an appointment for an interview. Ask the member of Congress how the campaign was conducted. Did the person challenge or fill a vacated seat? How were campaign funds raised? What campaign reforms would he or she like to see?

Self Test

After reading the assignment and watching the telelesson, you should be able to answer these questions. When you have completed the test, turn to the Answer Key to score your answers.

1. The constitutional requirements for a person running for the U.S. House of Representatives are to be
   a. a citizen for 7 years and at least 25 years old, and a resident of the state from which elected.
   b. a citizen for 7 years and resident of the state from which elected, and have voted in the last presidential election.
   c. a citizen for 7 years, at least 25 years old, and a resident of Washington, D.C.
   d. a resident of Washington, D.C., and at least 25 years old, and have served in the state legislature.

2. The constitutional requirements for a person running for the U.S. Senate are to be
   a. a citizen for 9 years, at least 30 years old, and a resident of Washington, D.C.
   b. a citizen for 9 years and a resident of the state from which elected, and have voted in the last presidential election.
   c. a citizen for 9 years, at least 30 years old, and a resident of the state from which elected.
   d. a resident of Washington, D.C., and at least 30 years old, and have served in the state legislature.

3. The Constitution states that U.S. representatives are to be elected every
   a. four years by popular vote.
   b. two years by popular vote.
   c. four years by the state legislatures.
   d. two years by the state legislatures.

4. The three major factors in determining who will run for congressional office are
   a. motivation, resources, and opportunity.
   b. relevance, money, and chance.
   c. drive, PACs, and luck.
   d. dedication, chance, and luck.

5. Those congressional elections held between presidential contests are called
   a. fall-term elections.
   b. coat-tail elections.
   c. midterm elections.
   d. post-term elections.

6. An incumbent has the advantage over a challenger through
   a. greater income and managerial experience.
   b. economic stability and political contacts.
   c. advanced age and a higher level of education.
   d. greater name identification and fund-raising ability.

7. If an incumbent has no serious challenger and continues to be re-elected time after time, the congressional district is called a
   a. hot seat.
   b. gerrymandered seat.
   c. powderpuff seat.
   d. safe seat.

8. The re-election goal is pursued in three major ways, by
   a. campaigning, debating, and fund raising.
   b. advertising, credit claiming, and position taking.
   c. electioneering, campaigning, and debating.
   d. debating, talking, and negotiating.

9. Which case held that, within each state, congressional districts must be approximately equal in population?
   a. *Baker v. Carr*
   b. *Wesberry v. Sanders*
   c. *Plessy v. Ferguson*
   d. *Reynolds v. Sims*

10. One of the most complicated aspects of congressional elections is reapportionment, which is
   a. the allocation of seats in the House to each state after each census and the redrawing of district boundaries within the state.
   b. the process that occurs when a member of the House files for election against an incumbent senator.
   c. a special election to fill a vacancy that has occurred within a state's congressional district.
   d. a court order to hold new elections, because the original election was invalidated due to voting irregularities.

11. There are several factors that influence a serious decision to run for the House or Senate, such as the
    a. candidate's access to media and support from family and friends.
    b. number of college-educated constituents and time of year for the primaries.
    c. time of year for the primaries and geographic size of the district.
    d. size of the candidate's family and the likelihood of endorsements.

12. Candidates must tap many sources for funds, such as
    a. wealthy friends to be individual contributors.
    b. everyone to whom the candidate has ever loaned money.
    c. every person who lives in the congressional district.
    d. corporations that seek favorable legislation.

13. The most critical aspect of modern campaigning, and by far the most expensive, is
    a. speech writers.
    b. campaign brochures.
    c. media advertising.
    d. direct mail.

14. Direct-mail appeals don't offer the glamour of television, but which of the following is one of the few ways they may NOT be equally effective?
    a. You can fashion a message for a particular audience.
    b. You can trace the donations from a particular audience.
    c. You can mail directly to a specific audience.
    d. You can say specifically what you want an audience to hear.

15. Since polling has become so critical in a congressional campaign, which of these is one of the few ways candidates do NOT use polling data?
    a. To shape strategy by determining what is important to voters
    b. To locate where support is strongest, undecided, or nonexistent
    c. To learn how many PACs have contributed
    d. To determine the candidate's chances of winning

16. A paid professional hired to devise a campaign strategy and manage a campaign is a
    a. political consultant.
    b. professional manager.
    c. political statistician.
    d. media expert.

17. A large number of candidates and elected officials began their own political careers as
    a. consultants.
    b. managers.
    c. volunteers.
    d. pollsters.

18. After the Watergate scandal, Congress passed new legislation
    a. limiting the time for campaigning.
    b. adjusting the term of office.
    c. limiting the raising and spending of campaign funds
    d. prohibiting the use of personal funds.

Short-Answer Question:
19. Describe what would make you participate more actively in a Senate or House campaign.

Answer Key

These are the correct answers with reference to the Learning Objectives, and to the source of the information: the Textbook Focus Points, Schmidt, *et al. American Government and Politics Today* (Schmidt), and the Telelesson Focus Points. Page numbers are also given for the Textbook Focus Points. "KT" indicates questions with Key Terms defined.

Question	Answer	Learning Objective	Textbook Focus Point (page no.)		Telelesson Focus Point
1	A	1	1 (Schmidt, pp. 303)		
2	C	1	1 (Schmidt, pp. 303)		
3	B	2	2 (Schmidt, pp. 390)		
4	A	1	3 (Schmidt, pp. 390)		
5	C	3	4 (Schmidt, pp. 392)	KT	
6	D	4	5 (Schmidt, pp. 392)		2
7	D	4	6 (Schmidt, pp. 394)		2
8	B	4	7 (Schmidt, pp. 392)		
9	B	5	8 (Schmidt, pp. 396)		
10	A	3	9 (Schmidt, pp. 396)	KT	1
11	A	1	3 (Schmidt, ppp. 390-391)		1
12	A	6			3
13	C	6			4
14	B	6			5
15	C	6		KT	6
16	A	6			7
17	C	6			8
18	C	5	8 (Schmidt, pp. 313-314)		9

Short Answer:

19		7		8

Lesson 14

Congress

Overview

Article I of the Constitution describes and lists the powers of the legislative branch of government: Congress. This lesson shows how the two houses are organized and who the leaders are. It also covers the committee system, in preparation for the next lesson on the legislative process.

At times in the history of the U.S. Congress, all of the power was held by a few senior members in leadership positions: the speaker of the House, the Senate majority leader, and the chairs of the standing committees. These few individuals decided the fate of most bills. But the reforms of the 1970s diffused congressional power. These reforms brought about needed changes, but they also created major stumbling blocks for legislation.

Another problem Congress faces is a negative public opinion of what it does—and doesn't—do. This is based in part on the small percentage of bills that it passes and a belief that Congress focuses on its own self interest and not on the interests of its constituents. An important part of this lesson addresses the public's role in the legislative process and examines how members of Congress gather information and opinions about pending legislation. If you and others like you are not participating in the legislative process, who is filling that void?

To better appreciate what members of Congress do, the television portion of the lesson follows a representative and a senator through the hectic schedule of a normal day. The intent of this lesson is to examine Congress and its operation, and to emphasize the responsibility that we all share for what Congress does and does not accomplish.

Learning Objectives

Goal: The purpose of "Congress" is to review the organization and structure of the House and Senate and to illustrate how representatives and senators integrate their own needs and those of their constituencies into their elected roles.

Objectives:

1. Explain the rationale for a bicameral Congress, cite the primary functions of Congress, and contrast the major similarities and differences between the House and the Senate.

2. Define and give examples of the "enumerated," or expressed, powers of Congress.

3. Outline two theories of representation to justify whether Congress is or is not truly a "constituent care" organization.

4. Describe the ethics questions facing Congress today, especially in the context of how the question of ethics may affect members' decisions about voting and handling "perks" and other privileges.

5 Explain the committee structure and formal leadership of the House and of the Senate.

6. Briefly describe what is required in order to prepare the national budget, and explain why the process is so complex.

7. Contrast the diffusion of power in Congress now with the way it was prior to the early 1970s, especially as this affects congressional operations.

8. Summarize the activities in a typical day in Washington, D.C., for a senator or representative, and note how these activities affect you.

Key Terms

Watch for these terms and pay particular attention to what each one means, as you follow the textbook and telelesson.

Bicameralism
Enumerated powers
"Necessary and proper"
  ("elastic") clause
Lawmaking
Trustees
Instructed delegates
Oversight
Rules committee
Filibustering
Cloture
Franking
Standing committee

Select committee
Joint committee
Conference committees
Seniority system
Safe seat
Speaker of the House
Majority Leader of the House
House Minority leader
Whips
President *pro tempore*
Senate majority floor leader
Senate minority floor leader

Textbook Reading Assignment

Schmidt, Shelley, and Bardes. *American Government and Politics Today*, 1993-94 edition. Chapter 12, "The Congress," pp. 377-390, 398-410, 414-421.

Textbook Focus Points

Before you read the textbook assignment, review the following points to help focus your thoughts. After you complete the assignment, write out your responses to reinforce what you have learned.

1. Why does the United States have a bicameral Congress?

2. What are "enumerated," or expressed, powers? List some of the enumerated powers of Congress.

3. What are the primary functions of Congress?

4. What are two theories of representation?

5. What are the major differences between the House and the Senate in terms of size, length of term, organization, and operation?

6. How can you decide if members of Congress truly represent you?

7. What are some of the perquisites ("perks") and other privileges of being a member of Congress?

8. How are the committees structured in the House and in the Senate?

9. What is the formal leadership of the House and the Senate?

10. How do members of Congress decide how to vote?

11. What all is involved in preparing the national budget?

12. How does the question of ethics affect Congress today?

Telelesson Interviewees

The following individuals share their expertise in the telelesson:

Thomas S. Foley–Democrat; U.S. Representative, State of Washington; Speaker of the House

Barbara Jordan–Professor, LBJ School of Public Affairs, University of Texas, Austin

Charles Percy–Republican; Former U.S. Senator, Illinois

Patricia Saiki–Republican; Former U.S. Representative, Hawaii

Mike Synar–Democrat; U.S. Representative, Oklahoma

Telelesson Focus Points

Before you view the telelesson, read over the following points to help focus your thoughts. After the presentation, write out your responses to help you remember these important points.

1. Who had real power in Congress before the early 1970s, and how was that power obtained?

2. How did the committee reforms of the 1970s diffuse, or spread, power in the House and in the Senate among more people?

3. How does this new diffusion of power affect the operation of Congress?

4. Is Congress a "constituent care" organization? How does this affect the relationship between the members of Congress and their constituents?

5. What is a typical day like in the life of a senator and a representative, and what parts of it benefit you?

Recommended Reading

The following suggestions are not required reading except when assigned by your instructor. They are listed to let you know where you can find additional information on areas which interest you.

Broder, David. "Who Took the Fun Out of Congress?" *The Washington Post Weekly Edition* (February 17, 1986).

Champagne, Anthony. *Congressman Sam Rayburn*. New Brunswick, N.J.: Rutgers University Press, 1984.

Miller, William M. *Fishbait: The Memoirs of the Congressional Doorkeeper*. Englewood Cliffs, N.J.: Prentice-Hall, 1977.

"The World of Congress." *Newsweek* (April 24, 1989): pp. 28-34.

Getting Involved

These activities are not required unless your instructor assigns them. But they offer good suggestions to help you understand and become more involved in the political process.

1. Note the "Getting Involved" section in your textbook at the end of Chapter 12.

2. Most members of Congress, especially House members, hold "town hall" meetings several times a year. Attend one to see how many constituents participate and what kind of questions they ask. Also note how the member of Congress uses staff members to handle constituent concerns.

Self Test

After reading the assignment and watching the telelesson, you should be able to answer these questions. When you have completed the test, turn to the Answer Key to score your answers.

1. Trying to balance the big states' population advantage and the small states' demand for equality, the founders created through the U.S. Constitution a(n)
    a. unicameral legislature.
    b. bicameral legislature.
    c. elite class.
    d. legislative assembly.

2. The enumerated powers of Congress are powers
    a. written into the U.S. Constitution.
    b. that Congress has given itself by passing laws.
    c. created by decisions of the Supreme Court.
    d. that are vague and often disputed by strong presidents.

3. Most constituents expect individual members of Congress to
    a. support legislation that is in the best interest of the country, regardless of its impact on their constituents.
    b. support the ideas of the member's political party.
    c. support the major ideas of the president.
    d. act as a broker between the needs of private citizens and the requirements of the federal government.

4. The two theories of representation are
    a. trustee and individualism.
    b. trustee and instructed delegate.
    c. individualism and instructed delegate.
    d. trustee and ombudsman.

5. One major difference between the House and the Senate is the number of members in each, which means that the
   a. House will spend more time than the Senate debating a bill on the floor.
   b. Senate can act on a bill more quickly than the House.
   c. House needs more rules.
   d. Senate is less experienced in debate.

6. Many members of the U.S. Senate and House of Representatives are not typical American citizens, because they are
   a. older and have more political experience than most Americans.
   b. younger than most Americans.
   c. more religious and less educated.
   d. nonwhite and female.

7. Members of Congress are granted generous franking privileges that
   a. permit them to mail letters without charge to their constituents.
   b. allow them to charge items to a special expense account.
   c. allow them unlimited calls to their district without charge.
   d. give them four round-trip air fares to their district each year.

8. Which one of the following does the committee structure NOT accomplish?
   a. It allows members to concentrate on a limited number of subjects.
   b. It restricts members' opportunity to give input.
   c. It provides for a division of labor in the legislature.
   d. It allows members to develop expertise in drafting legislation.

9. The formal leadership organization of Congress
    a. is strictly provided for in the Constitution.
    b. depends on the president.
    c. is based on political parties.
    d. has changed very little since the first Congress in 1789.

10. Most people who study the decision-making process in Congress
    agree that one of the best predictors for how a member will vote
    is his or her
    a. party membership.
    b. affiliation with organized interest groups.
    c. length of time in Congress.
    d. age and length of tenure.

11. The national budget is prepared by
    a. the president and the president's staff, then presented to
        Congress.
    b. the Senate majority leader, then presented to Congress.
    c. a bureaucratic agency, then presented to Congress.
    d. bureaucratic agencies, the president and presidential staff,
        and both chambers of Congress.

12. The most serious public-relations problem confronting Congress
    is
    a. its inability to defeat the president's legislative program.
    b. citizen concern about congressional ethics.
    c. the massive salary increases in the past four years.
    d. the lack of use of the War Powers Act during major
        foreign-policy disputes with the president.

13. For years, much of the power in Congress rested in
    a. select committees.
    b. conference committees.
    c. standing committees.
    d. interim committees.

14. The committee reforms of the 1970s broke the South's stranglehold on committee chairs by shifting the power from
    a. select committees to conference committees.
    b. senior committee members to freshman members.
    c. standing committees to subcommittees.
    d. conference committees to joint committees.

15. This new diffusion of power in Congress has
    a. added new layers of legislative interests.
    b. reduced the power of the president of the Senate.
    c. increased the pressure on the president.
    d. brought more cases to the Supreme Court.

16. Because members of Congress are concerned about being re-elected, which one of the following do they NOT try to do to keep their constituencies happy?
    a. Solve simple but visible problems for constituents
    b. Give the appearance of being responsible
    c. Accept large donations from rival organizations so as to hurt no one's feelings
    d. Return to their districts often to maintain close personal contact

Short-Answer Questions:
17. Give an overview of a typical day in the life of a senator or representative, and tell whether these actions reflect what you think a member of Congress ought to be doing.

18. Summarize what you see as the weaknesses of the House and the Senate.

19. Summarize what you see as the strengths of the House and the Senate.

Answer Key

These are the correct answers with reference to the Learning Objectives, and to the source of the information: the Textbook Focus Points, Schmidt, *et al. American Government and Politics Today* (Schmidt), and the Telelesson Focus Points. Page numbers are also given for the Textbook Focus Points. "KT" indicates questions with Key Terms defined.

Question	Answer	Learning Objective	Textbook Focus Point (page no.)		Telelesson Focus Point
1	B	1	1 (Schmidt, p. 380)	KT	
2	A	2	2 (Schmidt, p. 380)	KT	
3	D	1	3 (Schmidt, p. 382)		
4	B	3	4 (Schmidt, p. 383)	KT	
5	C	1	5 (Schmidt, p. 385)		
6	A	3	6 (Schmidt, p. 388)		4
7	A	4	7 (Schmidt, p. 399)	KT	
8	B	5	8 (Schmidt, p. 401)		3
9	C	5	9 (Schmidt, p. 405)		
10	A	4	10 (Schmidt, p. 410)		3
11	D	6	11 (Schmidt, p. 414)		
12	B	4	12 (Schmidt, p. 416)		
13	C	7	8 (Schmidt, p. 402)	KT	1
14	C	7			2
15	A	7			3
16	C	3			4

Short Answers:

17		8			5
18		1	5 (Schmidt, pp. 380-388)		2
19		1	5 (Schmidt, pp. 380-388)		2

The Legislative Process

Overview

A previous lesson examined the structure and leadership of the U.S. Congress. Here we investigate the legislative process itself.

This lesson gives you a chance to see Congress at work making new laws. It shows you how a bill becomes law by following two specific bills—the Civil Rights Act of 1991 and the Civil Liberties Act (better known as the Japanese Internment and Reparations Bill)—through the stages that a bill must go to become law.

Congress frequently is criticized for the low percentage of bills it passes. But Congress was designed to be a deliberative body, which makes a long road for a bill to travel from when it is first introduced in Congress to when it finally crosses the president's desk. People often point to the relatively small number of bills that eventually do become law as a sign that Congress doesn't accomplish much. But this low number also could indicate that Congress is closely scrutinizing bills and rejecting those that might not be in the best interests of the United States.

One of the major points this lesson makes is that people can influence the legislative process—either as individuals or as groups. The results may not be immediate; as we will see, it took Japanese-Americans interned during World War II over forty years to achieve any results. Yet without public involvement, there are many things Congress might never accomplish—or certainly not in the way we would want. Consequently, this lesson is designed to help you participate effectively in the legislative process, by pointing out the places along the legislative path where your input certainly can make a difference.

Learning Objectives

Goal: The purpose of "The Legislative Process" is to outline basic steps in lawmaking and describe the major factors that influence this process.

Objectives:

1. Describe the fate of a bill when the House and Senate pass different versions, when the president vetoes the bill, and when Congress overrides a presidential veto.

2. Illustrate the legislative process, using the Civil Rights Act of 1991 as an example.

3. State who can draft a bill and who can introduce it, and describe the basic steps a bill goes through to become a law.

4. Tell when and how an individual can affect the legislative process.

5. Explain the reasons why so few bills become law, including strategies that Congress and the president use to delay or stop passage of a bill.

Key Terms

Watch for these terms and pay particular attention to what each one means, as you follow the textbook and telelesson.

Subcommittee(TV)	Quorum call (TV)
Rules Committee(TV)	Veto (TV)
Conference committee(TV)	"Pocket veto" (TV)
Filibuster (TV)	Override (TV)

Textbook Reading Assignment

Schmidt, Shelley, and Bardes. *American Government and Politics Today,* 1993-94 edition. Chapter 12, "The Congress," pp. 410-414.

Textbook Focus Points

Before you read the textbook assignment, review the following points to help focus your thoughts. After you complete the assignment, write out your responses to reinforce what you have learned.

1. What happens when the House and Senate pass different versions of the same bill?

2. How may Congress override a presidential veto?

3. What happens to a bill if Congress overrides a presidential veto?

4. What does the passage of the Civil Rights Act of 1991 illustrate about the legislative process?

Telelesson Interviewees

The following individuals share their expertise in the telelesson:

Thomas Foley–Democrat; U.S. Representative, State of Washington; Speaker of the House
George Fujioki–Internment Camp Detainee
Mollie Fujioki–Internment Camp Detainee
Spark M. Matsunaga–Democrat; Former U.S. Senator, Hawaii

Telelesson Focus Points

Before viewing the telelesson, read over the following points to help focus your thoughts. After the presentation, write out your responses to help you remember these important points.

1. Who can draft a bill, and who can introduce this legislation?

2. What are the basic steps for a bill to become a law?

3. At which points in the legislative process can an individual influence a bill?

4. How can Congress and the president delay or stop passage of a bill?

5. Why do so few bills become law?

Recommended Reading

The following suggestions are not required reading unless your instructor assigns them. They are listed to let you know where you can find additional information on areas which interest you.

Alter, Jonathan, with Howard Fineman and Eleanor Clift. "World of Congress." *Newsweek* 113, no. 17 (April 24, 1989): pp. 26-34.

Keefe, William J. *The American Legislative Process: Congress and the States.* Englewood Cliffs, N.J.: Prentice-Hall, 1964.

Myer, Dillon S. *Uprooted American: The Japanese-American and the War Relocation Authority during World War II.* Tucson: University of Arizona Press, 1971.

Getting Involved

These activities are not required unless your instructor assigns them. But they offer good suggestions to help you understand and become more involved in the political process.

1. Choose a topic which you believe should be changed by legislation. Contact your state legislators and/or members of Congress about your concern and encourage them to introduce appropriate legislation.

2. Select a topic of interest about which legislation already has been introduced. Locate its present stage and follow the action until it is passed or defeated.

3. If you have access to C-SPAN, watch some of the U.S. House and Senate legislative activities and try to place the action on the legislative-process ladder.

Self Test

After reading the assignment and watching the telelesson, you should be able to answer these questions. When you have completed the test, turn to the Answer Key to score your answers.

1. Before bills can be sent to the president for signing, they must be
   a. signed by the majority leader of each house.
   b. passed by both houses in identical form.
   c. requested by the president.
   d. debated by a joint session of Congress.

2. Congress may override a presidential veto by
   a. an off-the record meeting with the president.
   b. a 51 percent vote in the conference committee.
   c. a two-thirds majority in both houses.
   d. a 51 percent vote in the House.

3. If Congress overrides a presidential veto, the bill
   a. receives a red flag.
   b. carries more importance.
   c. is delayed in implementation.
   d. becomes law without the president's signature.

---

4. Which of the following statements about the Civil Rights Act of 1991 does NOT illustrate a point about the legislative process?
   a. Declaring the law unconstitutional is the duty of the Supreme Court
   b. A complex issue requires a long time to be resolved
   c. Both sides had to compromise
   d. Interest groups played a part in the process

5. Legislation can be introduced in Congress only by
   a. the president.
   b. lobbyists.
   c. a senator or a representative.
   d. the secretary of state.

6. Once a bill has been introduced in Congress, it is assigned to a
   a. standing committee.
   b. conference committee.
   c. select committee.
   d. joint committee.

7. In which one of the following steps can an individual NOT influence the legislative process?
   a. Introducing the bill on the floor
   b. Testifying before the committee or subcommittee
   c. Lobbying members of Congress
   d. Encouraging the president to sign or veto the bill

8. Debate on a bill in the House is limited and controlled, but the Senate may extend a debate by
   a. requesting a change in a standing committee.
   b. using a filibuster.
   c. adjourning the debate.
   d. postponing a hearing.

Short-Answer Questions:

9. Describe the committee system's effect on the legislative process. Tell why the legislative process takes so long, and why so few bills become law.

10. List some advantages of the long and cumbersome legislative process.

11. The U.S. Constitution requires that both the House and the Senate must pass a particular bill in identical form. Describe how this requirement affects the relationship between the two chambers.

Answer Key

These are the correct answers with reference to the Learning Objectives, and to the source of the information: the Textbook Focus Points, Schmidt, *et al. American Government and Politics Today* (Schmidt), and the Telelesson Focus Points. Page numbers are also given for the Textbook Focus Points. "KT" indicates questions with Key Terms defined.

Question	Answer	Learning Objective	Textbook Focus Point (page no.)	Telelesson Focus Point
1	B	1	1 (Schmidt, p. 411)	
2	C	1	2 (Schmidt, p. 411) KT	
3	D	1	3 (Schmidt, p. 411) KT	
4	A	2	4 (Schmidt, p. 414)	
5	C	3		1
6	A	3	4 (Schmidt, p. 411)	2
7	A	4		3
8	B	5	KT	4

Short Answers:

9	5		5
10	5		5
11	1		2,4

The Presidency

Overview

Now it is time to add a second branch, the executive branch, to the three-branch structure of U.S. government. The president is head of the executive branch, which executes (administers or carries out) the laws passed by Congress, the legislative branch.

The executive branch is composed of the president, vice president, the president's cabinet, the Executive Office of the President, numerous independent regulatory agencies, and government corporations. (Another lesson will delve more into the plethora of government departments and agencies, as it describes the bureaucracy.)

Article II of the U.S. Constitution gives the president five powers: chief of state, chief executive, commander in chief, chief diplomat, and chief legislator. In addition to these five constitutional powers, the president is expected to fulfill several responsibilities just because he or she is president and the office requires it; these are called "inherent powers." We expect one individual to fulfill all the presidential roles, and we judge presidential success or failure by how well each president performs these roles.

Yet as our nation and our world have grown in size and complexity, being president of the United States has become much more difficult. Today, many people also consider it the most powerful position in the world. But, as a result of the almost superhuman challenges of the position, it is just about impossible for any one person to succeed in every area, or even to excel in several areas. What we have discovered is that some presidents will have great success performing one role, such as chief legislator, and fail in another, such as commander in chief.

Also due to the tremendous complexity of the job, presidents usually choose to emphasize one or two roles, and this choice influences the way they handle the job. Presidents cannot make decisions unchecked, for the founders designed a system of checks and balances to prevent one branch from becoming stronger than any other. However, this system creates conflict among the three branches, particularly between Congress and the president, which will be examined in the next lesson.

We as a nation are quick to criticize both presidential successes and presidential failures. On one hand we claim (or complain) that the presidency has become too powerful. On the other hand we say that the presidency is too weak. The more we learn about this massive job, the better able we become to evaluate what any one president does, and to cast our votes for the person best fitted to serve our nation at a particular time.

Learning Objectives

Goal: The purpose of "The Presidency" is to describe the organization and powers of the Executive Branch and to assess why a president will choose to emphasize one role over another.

Objectives:

1. Describe the constitutional requirements and personal considerations of individuals who aspire to become president of the United States.

2. List and explain the roles of the president, including acting as party chief, super politician, and television personality.

3. Discuss ways that presidents emphasize various roles and powers, using Lyndon Johnson and Jimmy Carter as examples.

4. Explain the impeachment process.

5. Describe the support the president receives from the Executive Office and the vice president.

6. Explain the high expectations the public holds for the president and the effect of these expectations on presidential performance.

7. Recount Helen Thomas's description of the presidency today and how the media have changed their coverage of the president.

8. Cite your opinion with supporting rationale as to whether the power of the presidency is increasing or decreasing.

Key Terms

Watch for these terms and pay particular attention to what each one means, as you follow the textbook and telelesson.

Chief of state   Emergency powers
Chief executive   Executive order
Appointment power   Executive privilege
Commander in Chief   Impeachment
Chief diplomat   Cabinet
Executive agreements   Executive Office of the President
Chief legislator   White House Office
State of the Union message   Council of Economic Advisers
Constitutional powers   Office of Management and Budget
Statutory powers   National Security Council
Express powers   Twenty-fifth Amendment
Inherent powers

Textbook Reading Assignment

Schmidt, Shelley, and Bardes. *American Government and Politics Today*, 1993-94 edition. Chapter 13, "The Presidency," pp. 423-461.

Textbook Focus Points

Before you read the textbook assignment, review the following points to help focus your thoughts. After you complete the assignment, write out your responses to reinforce what you have learned.

1. What are the qualifications to become president of the United States?

2. What are the five constitutional roles of the president and the functions of each?

3. In addition to the constitutional powers, what other powers does the president have?

4. What are the president's duties as party chief and super politician?

5. In what special ways have presidents used their powers?

6. How does the impeachment process work?

7. How is the Executive Office of the President organized?

8. How has the role of vice president as advisor and successor to the president evolved?

Telelesson Interviewees

The following individuals share their expertise in the telelesson:

George Christian–Former Press Secretary, Johnson Administration
Stuart Eizenstat–Chief Domestic Policy Advisor, Carter Administration
Kenneth Janda–Professor of Political Science, Northwestern University
Ron Nessen–Former Press Secretary, Ford Administration
Jody Powell–Former Press Secretary, Carter Administration
Helen Thomas–UPI White House Bureau Chief

Telelesson Focus Points

Before viewing the telelesson, read over the following points to help focus your thoughts. After the presentation, write out your responses to help you remember these important points.

1. Why does the public expect too much from the president, and how do these expectations influence how a president performs?

2. According to Jody Powell and Ron Nesson, what should the public realistically expect from a president, and why can't the president meet these expectations?

3. What roles did Lyndon Johnson and Jimmy Carter emphasize, and why?

4. How has television affected the presidency?

5. How does Helen Thomas describe both the presidency and how the media have changed in their coverage of the president?

6. Is the power of the presidency increasing or decreasing?

Recommended Reading

The following suggestions are not required unless your instructor assigns them. They are listed to let you know where you can find additional information on areas which interest you.

Barber, James David. *Presidential Character*, 3rd edition. Englewood Cliffs, N.J.: Prentice-Hall, 1985.

Cronin, Thomas E. "An Imperiled Presidency" in *The Post-Imperial Presidency*, Vincent Davis, editor. New Brunswick, N.J.: Transaction Books, 1980.

Schlesinger, Arthur. *The Imperial Presidency*. Boston: Houghton Mifflin, 1973.

Smith, Hedrick. "The Presidency and the Power Float: Our Rotating Prime Ministers" in *The Power Game*. New York: Random House, 1988, pp. 3-19.

Getting Involved

These activities are not required unless your instructor assigns them. But they offer good suggestions to help you understand and become more involved in the political process.

1. Note the "Getting Involved" section of your textbook at the end of Chapter 13.

2. Select a biography of a twentieth-century president. Read it to determine in which roles this person achieved the most success and in which roles, the least. Because of these successes and failures, did your opinion of this person change? Why?

Self Test

After reading the assignment and watching the telelesson, you should be able to answer these questions. When you have completed the test, turn to the Answer Key to score your answers.

1. Which of the following is NOT a constitutional requirement for becoming president of the United States?
   a. Must be a natural-born citizen
   b. Must be at least 35-years old
   c. Must have held an elective office
   d. Must have been a U.S. resident for 14 years

2. Which of the following is NOT a constitutional power of the president?
   a. Chief of state
   b. Chief of party
   c. Commander in chief
   d. Chief diplomat

3. Which of the following is NOT a type of presidential power?
   a. Constitutional power
   b. Statutory power
   c. Inherent power
   d. *De facto* power

4. One way the president has of exerting political power within the party is to
   a. write the party platform.
   b. appoint individuals to government or public jobs.
   c. control what the media print about the party leaders.
   d. determine committee assignments in Congress.

5. Which of the following is NOT a special use of presidential power?
   a. Impeachment power
   b. Emergency power
   c. Executive order
   d. Executive privilege

6. Article I of the U.S. Constitution authorizes the House and Senate to remove the president, vice president, or other civil officers of the United States for treason, bribery, or other high crimes and misdemeanors in a process called
   a. patronage.
   b. executive immunity.
   c. executive order.
   d. impeachment.

7. Under the Constitution, the organization of the executive branch
   a. includes a minimum of four cabinet-level departments.
   b. requires a constitutional amendment to change its structure.
   c. allows for numerous changes in the organization.
   d. cannot be changed more than once by each president.

8. The only formal duty for the vice president provided for in the Constitution is to
   a. preside over the Senate.
   b. represent the president at funerals.
   c. stand in for the president at official functions.
   d. give the opening speech when Congress convenes.

9. One reason the American people expect too much from a president is because the public
   a. expects the president to fulfill campaign promises.
   b. does not understand the five constitutional roles.
   c. is frustrated and wants someone to do something.
   d. bases its opinion of the president on George Washington.

10. Expectations that Jody Powell and Ron Nesson believe the public should have for the president do NOT include the idea that the president will
    a. set a clear direction for the country.
    b. try to keep world peace.
    c. try to reduce the threat of nuclear war.
    d. make sound economic decisions.

11. The urgency of urban and social problems required Lyndon Johnson to emphasize the role of chief
    a. executive.
    b. diplomat.
    c. of state.
    d. legislator.

12. In which of the following ways has television NOT affected the presidency?
    a. It has helped the president focus thoroughly on the issues.
    b. It has made the president more visible.
    c. It has influenced public perceptions of the president.
    d. It has changed the way we elect the president.

13. What one word does Helen Thomas use to describe the presidency?
    a. Intimidating
    b. Powerful
    c. Responsible
    d. Imperial

Short-Answer Question:
14. Do you believe that the power of the presidency is increasing or decreasing? Is this good or bad for the American people? Why?

Answer Key

These are the correct answers with reference to the Learning Objectives, and to the source of the information: the Textbook Focus Points, Schmidt, *et al. American Government and Politics Today* (Schmidt), and the Telelesson Focus Points. Page numbers are also given for the Textbook Focus Points. "KT" indicates questions with Key Terms defined.

Question	Answer	Learning Objective	Textbook Focus Point (page no.)	Telelesson Focus Point
1	C	1	1 (Schmidt, p. 425)	
2	B	2	2 (Schmidt, p. 429)	
3	D	2	3 (Schmidt, pp. 442-443)..KT	
4	B	2	4 (Schmidt, p. 443)	
5	A	3	5 (Schmidt, p. 445)	
6	D	4	6 (Schmidt, p. 447)..........KT	
7	C	5	7 (Schmidt, pp. 448-450)	
8	A	5	8 (Schmidt, p. 454)	
9	B	6		1
10	B	6		2
11	D	3	KT	3
12	A	2		4
13	B	7		5

Short Answer:

14		8	3 (Schmidt, pp. 458-459)	6

Lesson 17

The President and Congress

Overview

This lesson is one of a series of lessons on the Congress, the legislative process, and the presidency. Here we examine the deliberate and intentional conflict between the legislative and executive branches of government, and how it gets resolved.

The founders knew that the "checks and balances" which they built into the U.S. Constitution would mean a continuous battle for power and control. But they believed the struggle would be worth it in order to prevent one branch from becoming stronger than another.

Consequently, the conflict between Congress and the president is a natural outgrowth of our constitutional system. The president represents the entire nation and must look at national needs and concerns, whereas members of Congress represent a state, or a district within a state, and therefore offer a narrower geographical and socioeconomic perspective.

The checks and balances work like this: One constitutional role of the president is commander in chief, but only Congress can declare war. Congress makes all of the laws, but the president may veto them. The president may negotiate and sign a treaty, but the treaty is not valid unless the Senate approves (ratifies) it. The president appoints ambassadors, judges and cabinet officials, but they don't take office until the Senate consents to these appointments.

With all the conflict designed into the system, we may wonder what prevents a stalemate, a government that cannot act at all. The answer is that out of conflict comes some form of cooperation. Conflict causes Congress and the president to analyze the issues more closely, to maintain their stands on those provisions that are in what they perceive to be our best interests, and to discard those that might be less important or carry more risk.

In this lesson we look at two examples of conflict and cooperation: the budgetary responsibility and the war-making power. In the process we examine the powers that the Constitution gives each branch and see how both branches compromise to make our government work.

Learning Objectives

Goal: The purpose of "The President and Congress" is to illustrate the cooperation and conflict intentionally designed into the relationship between the legislative and executive branches of the U.S. government.

Objectives:

1. Outline the cooperative relationship and potential conflict between the president and Congress, as the president performs the constitutional roles of commander in chief, chief diplomat, and chief legislator.

2. Describe how special uses of presidential power create conflict between the president and Congress, particularly the Senate.

3. Illustrate conflict between the president and Congress, using the constitutional bases for budgetary responsibilities and war powers as examples, then show how the battles were resolved.

4. Explain the rationale of the founders in building conflict between the president and Congress into our governmental system.

Key Terms

Watch for these terms and pay particular attention to what each one means, as you follow the textbook and telelesson.

War Powers Act   Executive privilege
Advice and consent   Impeachment
Executive agreements   Impoundment (TV)
Veto message

Textbook Reading Assignment

Schmidt, Shelley, and Bardes. *American Government and Politics Today*, 1993-94 edition. Chapter 12, "The Congress," and Chapter 13, "The Presidency." [Review both chapters. In Chapter 12, focus on pp. 380-381, 410-416. In Chapter 13, pay particular attention to pp. 425-426, 429-443, 445-448.]

Textbook Focus Points

Before you read the textbook assignment, review the following points to help focus your thoughts. After you complete the assignment, write out your responses to reinforce what you have learned.

1. How has the War Powers Act affected the relationship between Congress and the president (as commander in chief)?

2. Where might conflict arise between Congress and the president when the president is performing the role of chief diplomat?

3. Where does conflict erupt between Congress and the president (as chief legislator)?

4. How can special uses of presidential power create conflict between Congress and the president?

Telelesson Interviewees

The following individuals share their expertise in the telelesson:

Thomas E. Cronin–Professor of Political Science, The Colorado College
William Gray–Democrat; Former U.S. Representative, Pennsylvania; Majority Whip; Former Chair of House Budget Committee
Andrea Mitchell–Chief Congressional Correspondent, NBC News
Charles Percy–Republican; Former Senator, Illinois
Elliot Richardson–Cabinet Member and Ambassador, Nixon and Ford Administrations

Telelesson Focus Points

Before viewing the telelesson, read over the following points to help focus your thoughts. After the presentation, write out your responses to help you remember these important points.

1. Why is there a conflict between Congress and the president over the budget?

2. What particularly causes conflict between the president and the Senate?

3. How can war-making powers create a conflict between the president and Congress?

4. Why was the conflict between the president and Congress built into our governmental system?

Recommended Reading

The following suggestions are not required unless your instructor assigns them. They are listed to let you know where you can find additional information on areas which interest you.

Borger, Gloria. "Storming the Tower." *U.S. News & World Report* 106 (March 6, 1989): pp. 37-39.

Cronin, Thomas E. *The State of the Presidency*, 2nd edition. Boston: Little, Brown, 1980.

Kernell, Samuel. *Going Public: New Strategies of Presidential Leadership*. Washington, D.C.: Congressional Quarterly Press, 1986.

Lamar, Jacob V. "Gone With the Wind." *Time* 130 (October 12, 1987): pp. 18-20.

Morganthau, T. "Tower's Troubles." *Newsweek* 113 (March 6, 1989): pp. 16-20+.

Press, Aric. "Bork in the Balance." *Newsweek* 110 (October 12, 1987): pp. 38-40.

Smith, Hedrick. "Divided Government: Gridlock and the Blame Game" in *The Power Game*. New York: Random House, 1988, pp. 651-667.

Getting Involved

These activities are not required unless your instructor assigns them. But they offer good suggestions to help you understand and become more involved in the political process.

1. In 1987 President Reagan nominated Robert Bork to the U.S. Supreme Court. This nomination encountered great opposition in the Senate and ultimately was defeated. Research Judge Bork's nomination and the Senate confirmation hearings: Who opposed the nomination and why? How did the administration react to the opposition? Pay careful attention to the conflict that arose when the president and Congress each performed their constitutional duties.

2. Select either the Special Watergate Committee of 1973 or the action by the House Judiciary Committee on articles of impeachment against President Richard Nixon in 1974. Examine news reports and books by participants. Look for the various points of conflict between the president and Congress.

Self Test

After reading the assignment and watching the telelesson, you should be able to answer these questions. When you have completed the test, turn to the Answer Key to score your answers.

1. In spite of the passage of the War Powers Act, the power of the president as commander in chief is
   a. virtually destroyed, with all real power belonging to the Joint Chiefs of Staff.
   b. much stronger than if it had not passed.
   c. increased, unless Congress declares war and takes control of the military.
   d. more extensive today than at any other time in our history.

2. The treaties negotiated and the ambassadors appointed by the president are worthless without
   a. diplomatic recognition by foreign powers.
   b. executive agreements with heads of foreign states.
   c. a State of the Union message by the president.
   d. the advice and consent of the Senate.

3. If the president uses a regular veto, the president must
   a. submit legislation that would accomplish the same goal through a different means.
   b. avoid using another regular veto for ten working days.
   c. obtain the approval of the majority leader in the Senate and the speaker of the House.
   d. return the bill to Congress with a veto message.

4. Presidents have at their disposal a variety of special powers and privileges which
   a. are not available to the other branches of U.S. government.
   b. have been carefully used with great discretion.
   c. Congress has tried to usurp.
   d. have been flaunted before Congress.

5. The Constitution specifically grants Congress the power to collect taxes, pay debts, and borrow money, whereas the president has
   a. sole responsibility for preparing the national budget.
   b. relinquished budgetary responsibility to Congress.
   c. no specific, constitutional, budgetary duties.
   d. always worked closely with Congress in developing a budget.

6. The Senate can assert itself over the president through
   a. denying the appointment of a federal judge.
   b. investigating the impeachment of a president.
   c. vetoing a president's proposal.
   d. impounding appropriated funds.

7. The War Powers Act has the effect of
   a. increasing the power and maneuverability of the president.
   b. decreasing the power and maneuverability of the president.
   c. making it easier for the president to work with Congress.
   d. making Congress appreciate the difficult job of being president.

8. According to Charles Percy, the founders wanted the president and Congress to share powers in order to
   a. protect the people and remove the possibility of autocracy.
   b. generate an attitude of cooperation among all the states.
   c. create a sense of "unitedness" among the individual states.
   d. stimulate a thorough examination of the issues before setting policies.

Short-Answer Question:
9. Do you believe that Congress should place constraints on the president? Why or why not?

Answer Key

These are the correct answers with reference to the Learning Objectives, and to the source of the information: the Textbook Focus Points, Schmidt, *et al. American Government and Politics Today* (Schmidt), and the Telelesson Focus Points. Page numbers are also given for the Textbook Focus Points. "KT" indicates questions with Key Terms defined.

Question	Answer	Learning Objective	Textbook Focus Point (page no.)	Telelesson Focus Point
1	D	1	1 (Schmidt, p. 434)	KT
2	D	1	2 (Schmidt, p. 434)	KT
3	D	1	3 (Schmidt, p. 439)	KT
4	A	2	4 (Schmidt, p. 449)	
5	C	3		1
6	A	2	2 (Schmidt, p. 431)	2
7	B	3	1 (Schmidt, p. 434)	KT 3
8	A	4		4

Short Answer:

9		4	1,2,3,4 (Schmidt, pp. 427-443)	1,2,3,4

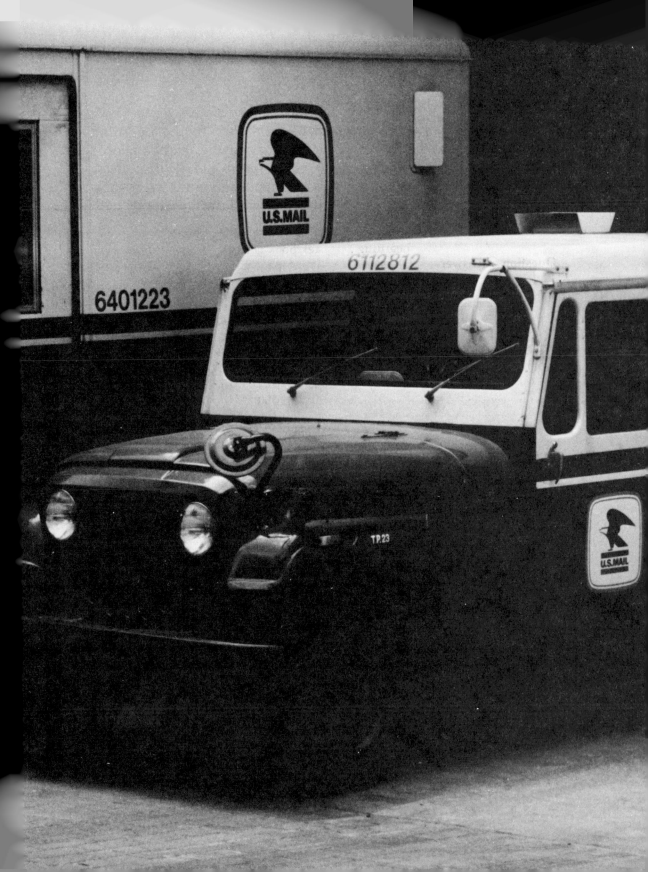

Lesson 18

The Bureaucracy

Overview

What comes to your mind when you hear the terms "bureaucracy" or "red tape"? When we asked this question, most people answered with such terms as "big," "wasteful," "inefficient," and "frustrated"—just to name a few. If you remember some of the candidates' promises from the last several presidential campaigns, you probably recall that most candidates promised to clean up the bureaucracy. These were not idle promises; their intentions were good. But were they able to achieve any results?

This lesson looks at the bureaucracy with an unbiased eye and identifies its role in our governmental process. We define bureaucracy, investigate its functions, and see how well it performs these functions.

Then we turn our attention to how the National Park Service, part of the U.S. Department of Interior, fought the massive forest fires that burned across the western states in 1988 by enforcing the policies that had been developed for such occasions. Due to public outcry, pressure on politicians, and media attention, these policies were slowly changed—proving that federal agencies do respond to criticism.

Next, we consider the Internal Revenue Service, without doubt one of the most pervasive—some say invasive—of all federal agencies, as it affects virtually everyone who lives in the United States. The IRS exemplifies all the characteristics of a bureaucracy, both good and bad. But it too can change, as it did in 1988 after Congress passed the "Taxpayers' Bill of Rights."

The U.S. bureaucracy has become so large and affects so many areas of our lives that it has been called "the fourth branch of government." It is massive, but we also ask it to perform herculean tasks—such as delivering the mail all across the United States in every kind of climatic condition for under 50 cents. Given the role that government plays in our lives, we need to understand how and why the bureaucracy works as it does. Then, when changes are necessary, we will know how and where to begin!

Learning Objectives

Goal: The purpose of "The Bureaucracy" is to assess the extent to which the bureaucracy responds to our needs, and to recognize when and how the bureaucracy should be held accountable or changed.

Objectives:

1. Outline strategies used by Congress and the president to control our bureaucracies, often called the "permanent government."

2. Define "bureaucracy" and list some of the activities it does well and some, not so well.

3. Describe how the organization and staffing of the federal bureaucracy has evolved, emphasizing its phenomenal growth.

4. Analyze recent attempts to reform the federal bureaucracy and make it more accountable.

5. Explain the roles that bureaucrats play as politicians, policymakers, and nonpolitical public servants.

6. List some ways that individuals can deal effectively with the federal bureaucracy.

7. Illustrate the typical responsiveness of the bureaucracy, using the examples of the National Park Service fighting forest fires in 1988 and the Internal Revenue Service participating in tax reform.

Key Terms

Watch for these terms and pay particular attention to what each one means, as you follow the textbook and telelesson.

Bureaucracy
Cabinet departments
Independent executive agency
Independent regulatory agency
Government corporation
Spoils system
Merit system
Pendleton Act

Civil Service Commission
Hatch Act
Government in the
   Sunshine Act
Sunset legislation
Whistle-blower
Iron triangle

Textbook Reading Assignment

Schmidt, Shelley, and Bardes. *American Government and Politics Today*, 1993-94 edition. Chapter 14, "The Bureaucracy," pp. 463-491.

Textbook Focus Points

Before you read the textbook assignment, review the following points to help focus your thoughts. After you complete the assignment, write out your responses to reinforce what you have learned.

1. How successful have presidents been in controlling or changing the federal bureaucracy?

2. What is a bureaucracy, and what are some of its characteristics?

3. How is the federal bureaucracy organized?

4. How has the staffing of the federal bureaucracy evolved?

5. What are some recent attempts to reform the federal bureaucracy?

6. How do bureaucrats play the roles of politicians and policymakers, when they are supposed to be nonpolitical?

7. How does Congress try to control the federal bureaucracy?

Telelesson Interviewees

The following individuals share their expertise in the telelesson:

Gary A. Booth–Director, Dallas District, Internal Revenue Service

Brad Leonard–Acting Director, Office of Program Analysis, U.S. Department of Interior

Peter Woll–Professor of Political Science, Brandeis University

Sherman Wyman–Professor, Institute of Urban Studies, University of Texas, Arlington

Telelesson Focus Points

Before viewing the telelesson, read over the following points to help focus your thoughts. After the presentation, write out your responses to help you remember these important points.

1. What is the estimated size of the federal bureaucracy, and why has it grown so?

2. What types of activities does the bureaucracy do well and not so well?

3. How can individuals deal effectively with the federal bureaucracy?

4. Why is the bureaucracy often called the "permanent government," and how does this permanency affect the operation of government?

5. How does the example of the National Park Service fighting forest fires in 1988 illustrate the way bureaucracies operate?

6. How does the Internal Revenue Service typify a classic bureaucracy, and what has been done to make it more responsive?

7. To whom is the bureaucracy accountable, and when and by whom should it be called to account for its actions?

Recommended Reading

The following suggestions are not required unless your instructor assigns them. They are listed to let you know where you can find additional information on areas which interest you.

Alter, Jonathan. "The Powers that Stay" in Peter Woll's *Behind the Scenes in American Government: Personalities and Politics*, 6th edition. Boston: Little, Brown and Company, 1987, pp. 354-364.

"Congress Has Leveled the Playing Field for Contests with the Tax Man." *U.S. News & World Report* 106 (March 27, 1989): p.79.

Woll, Peter. "Constitutional Democracy and Bureaucratic Power" in *Public Administration and Policy*. Boston: Little, Brown and Company, 1966, pp. 1-14.

"Your Rights as a Taxpayer." *Consumers Research Magazine* 72 (March 1989): pp. 20-24.

Getting Involved

These activities are not required unless your instructor assigns them. But they offer good suggestions to help you understand and become more involved in the political process.

1. Visit your local post office and ask the officials to show you how a letter gets from your home mail box to its final destination. If you live in a large city, you might like to go to both your own branch and the main post office, to see the total picture. Ask the people with whom you talk to estimate how much a private company would charge to deliver the same letter.

2. Note the "Getting Involved" section in your textbook at the end of Chapter 14.

3. Most of us have to file an income tax report each year. To learn how your report is processed, contact a local Internal Revenue Service office and ask for an official to explain to you the normal procedure for processing a claim.

Self Test

After reading the assignment and watching the telelesson, you should be able to answer these questions. When you have completed the test, turn to the Answer Key to score your answers.

1. Presidential attempts to affect significantly the structure and operation of the federal bureaucracy are
   a. very successful.
   b. a result of hard work that is now beginning to pay off.
   c. generally unsuccessful.
   d. worthwhile when Congress has been controlled by Democrats.

2. Bureaucracy is the name given to any
   a. large branch of a government that has power to make laws.
   b. organization that has major problems when attempting to accomplish its goals.
   c. group of people who work together to enforce policies in a way that prevents quick results.
   d. large organization that is structured hierarchically and is supposed to carry out specific functions.

3. Which one of the following is NOT a major type of bureaucratic structure?
   a. Cabinet departments
   b. Copyright Royalty Tribunal
   c. Independent executive agencies
   d. Independent regulatory agencies

4. The president is able to make political appointments to most of the top jobs in the federal bureaucracy, but the rest of the individuals who work for the national government got their jobs through
   a. the merit system of the civil service department.
   b. appointment based on membership in the natural aristocracy.
   c. helping get the president elected and relying on the spoils system.
   d. passing a battery of tests and applying through Congress.

---

5. Which of the following is NOT a recent attempt at reforming the federal bureaucracy?
   a. Privatization
   b. Sunshine and sunset laws
   c. Protection for whistle-blowers
   d. Department of Veteran Affairs

6. A realistic view of the role of the bureaucracy in policymaking is that agencies and departments of government
   a. play a neutral role in making policy.
   b. provide only relevant information to the policymakers.
   c. administer without attempting to influence policies.
   d. play an important role in making policy.

7. The ultimate check that Congress has over the bureaucracy is the ability to
   a. hire and fire members of boards and commissions.
   b. write legislation in terms so vague that the bureaucracy will not be able to interpret the meaning.
   c. withhold appropriations of money to the bureaucracy.
   d. influence the president to take action against a bureaucrat.

8. Which of the following reasons does NOT account for the continued growth of the federal bureaucracy?
   a. New technological advancements
   b. New policies set by new presidents
   c. New laws enacted by Congress
   d. Increases in the nation's population

9. According to Sherman Wyman, which of the following activities does a bureaucracy NOT do well?
   a. Provide a valuable financial resource
   b. Provide a water supply
   c. Provide a fascinating career arena
   d. Provide police and fire protection

10. Sherman Wyman recommends that individuals deal with the bureaucracy by
    a. being dogmatic in order not to give the bureaucracy an opportunity to respond.
    b. researching a request much as you would if applying for a federal grant.
    c. defending your position so that you cannot be accused of being negligent.
    d. approaching the bureaucracy much as you would approach a friend or any other group of people.

11. Presidents, members of Congress, and some federal judges come and go, but most of the bureaucrats remain on the job–causing the bureaucracy to be referred to as the
    a. government in the sunshine.
    b. permanent government.
    c. government corporation.
    d. seniority system.

12. The actions of the National Park Service during the 1988 forest fires typify the bureaucracy, because the
    a. head of the agency inspected the area before action was taken.
    b. new fire fighters hired to fight the fires were terminated.
    c. Park Service was very slow to change its policies.
    d. strategies were carefully mapped out with input from many agencies.

13. Which of the following traits of the Internal Revenue Services does NOT typify the classic traits of a bureaucracy?
    a. Large size
    b. Complex organization
    c. Strict compliance to rules
    d. Adaptable to change

14. Bureaucratic experts like Peter Woll believe the bureaucracy should be accountable to the
    a. public through our elected officials.
    b. media through their power to report the news.
    c. president as the chief executive.
    d. cabinet directors who head the various agencies.

Short-Answer Question:

15. If you were an incoming president, what reforms would you recommend for the federal bureaucracy and how would you implement them?

Answer Key

These are the correct answers with reference to the Learning Objectives, and to the source of the information: the Textbook Focus Points, Schmidt, *et al. American Government and Politics Today* (Schmidt), and the Telelesson Focus Points. Page numbers are also given for the Textbook Focus Points. "KT" indicates questions with Key Terms defined.

Question	Answer	Learning Objective	Textbook Focus Point (page no.)	Telelesson Focus Point
1	C	1	1 (Schmidt, p. 465)	
2	D	2	2 (Schmidt, p. 465)	KT
3	B	3	3 (Schmidt, p. 469)	
4	A	3	4 (Schmidt, p. 475)	
5	D	4	5 (Schmidt, p. 481)	
6	D	5	6 (Schmidt, p. 485)	
7	C	1	7 (Schmidt, p. 486)	
8	A	3		1
9	A	2		2
10	D	6		3
11	B	1		4
12	C	7		5
13	D	7		6
14	A	4		7

Short Answer:

15		4		7

SOCIAL SECURITY
XXX-XX-XXXX
THIS NUMBER HAS BEEN ESTABLISHED FOR
JOHN DOE
SIGNATURE

Lesson 19

Domestic Policy

Overview

This lesson brings together every component of the governmental process that we have studied so far: the constitutional basis, the participation of the people through interest groups and political parties, the process of electing a president and members of Congress, the political institutions of Congress and the presidency, the legislative process, and the federal bureaucracy. All of these elements must cooperate to produce a product, such as domestic policy or foreign policy.

In looking at the legislative process, we followed the steps to pass a bill and sign it into law. In our study of the bureaucracy, we found out how a law is turned into policy. Now we define domestic policy: all of the national laws and actions that affect life within the nation's borders. Since the president and Congress are responsible for making domestic policy, we examine the basic steps in developing such a policy: building, formulating, adopting, implementing, and evaluating an agenda.

Next, we find out how various kinds of domestic policy are implemented. To accomplish this, we look at an agency that affects almost every one of us, either through the taxes we pay to it or the benefits we receive from it: the Social Security Administration. In the process we see the concept and costs of trade-offs in action.

With 535 members of Congress representing the 50 states, everybody wants something; there is an infinite number of requests for a finite amount of resources. This situation produces another kind of trade-off: We increase the amount of funds spent on welfare but reduce what is spent on the environment; we increase military spending but reduce aid to education. The textbook calls this an "action-reaction syndrome."

Basically, we must realize that setting domestic policy is an ongoing process, and one that is constantly open to change. In addition, we are continually faced with numerous problems in search of solutions; there rarely is consensus on how these problems should be solved. Consequently, we need to voice our concerns and become actively involved in affecting the decision-making process. For only then will we have a say in the policies that affect us.

Learning Objectives

Goal: The purpose of "Domestic Policy" is to illustrate how the legislative and executive branches produce domestic policy, which affects us all.

Objectives:

1. Explain the policy-making process from the time a nation or state becomes aware of a problem requiring government attention, through the final implementation and enforcement of action on it by the bureaucracy.

2. Show how the way that domestic policy is carried out affects individuals, specifically the lack of comprehensive health-care, the increase of poverty and homelessness, environmental policy, and the concern for public safety and crime.

3. Describe processes used by Congress to determine domestic priorities and how congressional oversight affects the setting of the national agenda.

4. Illustrate the implementation of domestic policy, citing the 1987 funding package for the Department of Transportation and resolution of the social security crisis of the early 1980s as examples.

Key Terms

Watch for these terms and pay particular attention to what each one means, as you follow the textbook and telelesson.

Policy trade-offs National agenda (TV)
Social Security Domestic policy (TV)
Income transfer

Textbook Reading Assignment

Schmidt, Shelley, and Bardes. *American Government and Politics Today*, 1993-94 edition. Chapter 16, "Politics of Economic Policy Making," pp. 529-537, 554, and Chapter 17, "Domestic Policy," pp. 557-591.

Textbook Focus Points

Before you read the textbook assignment, review the following points to help focus your thoughts. After you complete the assignment, write out your responses to reinforce what you have learned.

1. How does a nation or state become aware of a problem that governments need to address, and how is a solution found?

2. How does the American government address the problems of health-care, poverty, and homelessness?

3. How has the government reacted to environmental problems?

4. How does the government handle the problems of public safety and crime in America?

5. How does the American government combat the drug problem?

Telelesson Interviewees

The following individuals will share their expertise in the telelesson:

Thomas S. Foley–Democrat; U.S. Representative, State of Washington; Speaker of the House

William Gray–Democrat; Former U.S. Representative, Pennsylvania; House Majority Whip

Don P. Watson–Regional Administrator, Southwest Region, Federal Aviation Administration

Aaron Wildavsky–Professor of Political Science and Public Policy, University of California, Berkley

Telelesson Focus Points

Before viewing the telelesson, read over the following points to help focus your thoughts. After the presentation, write out your responses to help you remember these important points.

1. What are "domestic policy" and "national agenda," and how are they determined?

2. Explain how the 1987 funding package for the Department of Transportation was developed.

3. According to Aaron Wildavsky, how is American domestic policy made and what changes are needed in the process?

4. What was the social security crisis in the early 1980s, and how was it resolved?

5. According to William Gray, what are the consequences of social security benefits being "untouchable"?

6. How does Tom Foley say Congress determines domestic priorities?

7. How does congressional oversight affect domestic policy?

Recommended Reading

The following suggestions are not required unless your instructor assigns them. But they are listed to let you know where you can find additional information on areas which interest you.

Anderson, Harry. "The Social Security Crisis." *Newsweek* 101 (January 24, 1983): pp. 18-23+.

Harrington, Michael. *The New American Poverty*. New York: Penguin Books, 1985.

Hildreth, James M. "Social Security Rescue–What It Means to You." *U.S. News & World Report* 94 (April 4, 1983): pp. 23-25.

Peterson, Peter G. "Can Social Security Be Saved?" *Reader's Digest* 122 (March 1983): pp. 49-54.

Wohl, Burton. *China Syndrome*. New York: Bantam Books, 1979.

Getting Involved

These activities are not required unless your instructor assigns them. But they offer good suggestions to help you understand and become more involved in the political process.

1. Note the "Getting Involved" section of your textbook at the end of Chapter 16 and Chapter 17.

2. Contact a federal agency in your area, such as the Social Security Administration or the Food and Drug Administration, to learn what domestic-policy programs are being implemented by that agency. Find out how that agency affects you.

Self Test

After reading the assignment and watching the telelesson, you should be able to answer these questions. When you have completed the test, turn to the Answer Key to score your answers.

1. The concept of agenda adoption refers to the
    a. specific strategy being selected from among the various proposals discussed.
    b. final compromise between Congress and the executive branch.
    c. policy disputes mediated by the Office of Management and Budget.
    d. specific plan of action from the Congressional Budget Office.

2. One factor that effects the changing demographics of our population is
    a. Ellis Island is now closed to immigrants.
    b. U.S. Immigration Service has been dismantled.
    c. the U.S. population is getting older.
    d. the population continues to move to the suburbs.

3. Which of the following groups is NOT included among the "new poor"?
    a. Single-parent families
    b. Rainbow coalition
    c. Youth
    d. Single elderly people

4. The National Environmental Policy Act of 1969 did NOT
   a. establish the Council for Environmental Quality.
   b. mandate that an environmental impact statement be prepared for every action affecting the quality of the environment.
   c. require a feasibility study accompany each request for federal funds for environmental projects.
   d. give citizens a weapon against the government for unnecessary & inappropriate use of resources.

5. What most Americans are worried about is
   a. violent crime.
   b. catastrophic events.
   c. nuclear attack.
   d. financial collapse.

6. What is considered the major source of America's public safety crisis?
   a. Traffic violations
   b. Gangs
   c. Illegal drugs
   d. Unregulated gun control

7. Those things that the national government does and does not do to make our society a better place to live make up this nation's
   a. agenda.
   b. domestic policy.
   c. public assistance.
   d. social insurance.

8. In the formulation of the Department of Transportation funding package, questions related to
   a. what the total amount would be for the department to plan its projects.
   b. which section of the budget the package would be placed.
   c. who would administer the funds: the national government or the states.
   d. which specific items would be cut to help reduce the federal deficit.

9. According to Aaron Wildavsky, U.S. domestic policy is made by the
   a. special interest groups who lobby Congress.
   b. president because he represents the interests of the entire nation.
   c. military because it doesn't want funds removed from foreign policy.
   d. people who are elected for that purpose.

10. Because people were living longer and receiving benefits for a longer period of time, and because benefits were increased without raising taxes, the social security system in the early 1980s was almost
    a. bankrupt.
    b. solvent.
    c. volatile.
    d. prosperous.

11. According to William Gray, the untouchability of social security benefits takes a significant chunk out of the national budget, which means that deficit reduction must
    a. be addressed before finalizing the budget.
    b. be taken out of the military budget.
    c. come out of other programs.
    d. become a priority item on the national agenda.

12. Which of the following is NOT one of the questions that Tom Foley says must be answered in order for Congress to set priorities and reach a consensus on the budget resolution?
    a. Where should the country go?
    b. Who should implement the country's goals?
    c. How many resources should be applied to reach goals?
    d. What kinds of resources should be applied to reach goals?

Short-Answer Question:
13. How does congressional oversight affect domestic policy?

Answer Key

These are the correct answers with reference to the Learning Objectives, and to the source of the information: the Textbook Focus Points, Schmidt, *et al. American Government and Politics Today* (Schmidt), and the Telelesson Focus Points. Page numbers are also given for the Textbook Focus Points. "KT" indicates questions with Key Terms defined.

Question	Answer	Learning Objective	Textbook Focus Point (page no.)	Telelesson Focus Point
1	A	1	1 (Schmidt, p. 532)	
2	C	2	2 (Schmidt, p. 560)	
3	B	2	2 (Schmidt, p. 567)	
4	C	2	3 (Schmidt, pp. 574-575)	
5	A	2	4 (Schmidt, p. 583)	
6	C	2	5 (Schmidt, p. 584)	
7	B	3		KT 1
8	D	4		2
9	D	3		KT 3
10	A	4		4
11	C	4		5
12	B	3		6

Short Answer:

13		4	1 (Schmidt, pp. 531-533)	KT 7

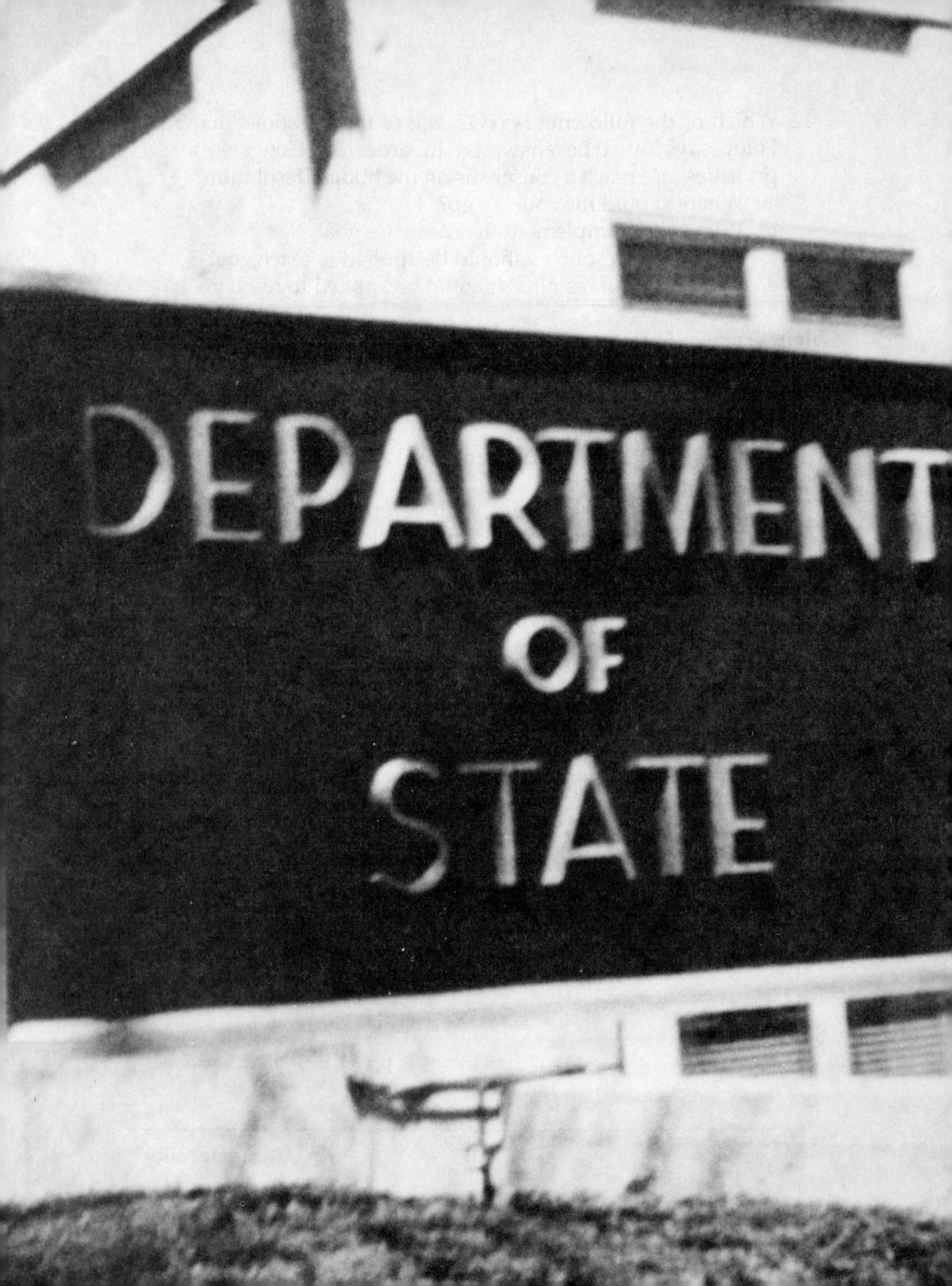
DEPARTMENT
OF
STATE

Lesson 20

Foreign Policy

Overview

This lesson on making policy differs from the lesson on domestic policy, because here we look at how the U.S. government makes decisions that affect our country's relationships with other countries. Just as domestic policy is an ongoing process, so too is foreign policy. In addition, the concept of trade-offs is as relevant here as it is with domestic policy. Finally, both domestic and foreign policy require negotiation; the difference is that foreign policy must be made with a world neighborhood in mind.

Not too long ago, when we heard the term "foreign policy," we envisioned guns, tanks, and battleships fighting wars. To a large degree, this vision still holds true. So we first examine the war-making powers and duties of both the president and Congress. We study tools the president uses to make these foreign-policy decisions, such as the departments of State and Defense, National Security Council, and Central Intelligence Agency. We also investigate various foreign-policy themes the United States has employed, defining "cold war," "containment," and "detente."

But recently another element has entered the picture: the economy of a nation that relies heavily on foreign trade. We examine the new economic component of foreign policy through a case study dealing with Western Europe and Japan. In the process we question experts about both the trade and the military policies that exist between these areas and the United States, as well as how and why these policies were chosen.

Because the nations of the world are interdependent, one nation's policies can, and usually do, affect the policies of other nations. The effects of the deluge of Japanese cars on the U.S. automotive industry illustrates this well.

Learning Objectives

Goal: The purpose of "Foreign Policy" is to describe why and how the United States develops and implements foreign policy in an interdependent world.

Objectives:

1. Describe U.S. foreign policy–what it is; who makes it; what issues affect it; and its philosophy, major themes, and current challenges.

2. Outline the limitations on a president's war-making powers and what attempts have been made to reduce the nuclear threat.

3. List non-government sources which affect U.S. foreign policy.

4. Compare U.S. trade policy with that of western Europe and of Japan.

5. Contrast U.S. military policy toward western Europe with that toward Japan.

6. Describe how U.S. foreign policy with regard to western Europe and to Japan affects individuals in this country.

Key Terms

Watch for these terms and pay particular attention to what each one means, as you follow the textbook and telelesson.

Foreign policy
Diplomacy
Economic aid
Technical assistance
National security policy
National Security Council
Moral idealism
Political realism
Executive agreement

Intelligence community
Military-industrial complex
Monroe Doctrine
Cold war
Iron curtain
Containment
Detente
Trade deficit (TV)
European Economic Community (TV)

Textbook Reading Assignment

Schmidt, Shelley, and Bardes. *American Government and Politics Today*, 1993-94 edition. Chapter 18, "Foreign and Defense Policy," pp. 593-627.

Textbook Focus Points

Before you read the textbook assignment, review the following points to help focus your thoughts. After you complete the assignment, write out your responses to reinforce what you have learned.

1. What is foreign policy?

2. What has been America's philosophy in foreign policy?

3. Who makes foreign policy?

4. How have the president's war-making powers been limited?

5. What non-governmental sources may influence foreign policy?

6. What have been the major themes of American foreign policy?

7. What are some of the contemporary world problems which affect American foreign policy?

Telelesson Interviewees

The following individuals share their expertise in the telelesson:

Gerald Curtis–Director of East Asian Institute, Columbia University
Marvin Kalb–Professor, Center for Press, Politics, and Public Policy, Harvard University
Rozanne Ridgeway–Assistant Secretary of State, Bureau of European and Canadian Affairs, U.S. Department of State

Telelesson Focus Points

Before viewing the telelesson, read over the following points to help focus your thoughts. After the presentation, write out your responses to help you remember these important points.

1. Who makes foreign policy for the United States?

2. What is the challenge facing today's foreign-policy makers?

3. Describe the U.S. trade policy with western Europe.

4. Describe the U.S. military policy with regard to western Europe.

5. Describe the U.S. trade policy with Japan.

6. Describe the U.S. military policy with regard to Japan.

7. What problems has the United States had with Japan over economic policy?

8. According to Marvin Kalb, how does U.S. foreign policy regarding western Europe and Japan affect us as individuals?

Recommended Reading

The following suggestions are not required unless your instructor assigns them. They are listed to let you know where you can find additional information on areas which interest you.

Alm, Richard. "That Intractable Trade Deficit." *U.S. News & World Report* 101 (September 15, 1986): p. 42.

Clancy, Tom. *Red Storm Rising*. New York: G.P. Putnam's Sons, 1986.

Crabb, Cecil V., and Pat M. Holt. *Invitation to Struggle: Congress, the President and Foreign Policy*. Washington, D.C.: Congressional Quarterly Press, 1980.

Friedman, Milton. "Straight Talk about Deficits." *Reader's Digest* 134 (March 1989): pp. 105-107.

Hattori, Ichiro. "Trade Conflicts: A Japanese View." *Vital Speeches of the Day* 52 (January 15, 1986): pp. 218-221.

Norton, Robert E., and Jack Egan. "Manufacturing a Trade Gap." *U.S. News & World Report* 104 (May 16, 1988): pp.38-39.

Rudolph, Barbara. "A Baffling Trade Imbalance." *Time* 128 (August 11, 1986): pp. 40-42.

Rudolph, Barbara. "Punch in the Eye." *Time* 131 (April 25, 1988): pp. 58-59.

Samuelson, Robert J. "Japan's Case of Malaise." *Newsweek* 109 (May 4, 1987): p.47.

Getting Involved

These activities are not required unless your instructor assigns them. But they offer good suggestions to help you understand and become more involved in the political process.

1. Take a trip to a local variety store or department store. Inspect the labels on a number of items to determine how many are imported and how many are American-made. Closer to home, look around your own home: What kind of car do you drive? What kind of television do you watch? Keep a record, then tally how much you are subtracting from or contributing to the U.S. trade deficit.

2. Note the "Getting Involved" section of your textbook at the end of Chapter 18.

Self Test

After reading the assignment and watching the telelesson, you should be able to answer these questions. When you have completed the test, turn to the Answer Key to score your answers.

1. Foreign policy refers to
   a. the goals a nation wants to achieve, and the techniques and strategies used in trying to achieve them.
   b. formal agreements between nations, which are approved by the World Court.
   c. all actions with other countries that are not related to economics.
   d. only the treaties and executive agreements that are ratified by the Senate.

2. From the earliest years of the republic, Americans have felt that their nation
   a. should have diplomatic ties with every nation.
   b. supplied economic aid to its needy neighbors.
   c. provided technical assistance as we developed it.
   d. had a special destiny.

3. The Constitution created an "invitation to struggle" for control over the foreign-policy process between the
   a. National Security Council and the president.
   b. Department of State and the National Security Council.
   c. president and Congress.
   d. Department of State and Congress.

4. In principle, the State Department is the executive agency that is
   a. directly responsible to Congress.
   b. not involved in short-term foreign policy.
   c. most directly involved with foreign affairs.
   d. responsible for making foreign policy, not the president.

5. In 1973, Congress passed the War Powers Act which
   a. bestowed power on Congress concerning all military actions.
   b. limited the president's use of troops in military action without congressional approval.
   c. extended the president's power to deploy troops as military crises developed.
   d. recognized the increased threat of nuclear war.

6. Which of the following non-governmental sources does NOT influence U.S. foreign policy?
   a. The elite and mass opinion
   b. The military-industrial complex
   c. U.S. multinational business enterprises
   d. The Federal Communications Commission

7. Which of the following has NOT been a major theme of American foreign policy?
   a. Isolationism
   b. Interventionism
   c. Aversion
   d. Internationalism

8. Which of the following is NOT considered a challenge for U.S. foreign policy?
   a. Foreign trade to mainland China
   b. End of the Cold War
   c. Dissolution of the Soviet Union
   d. Political changes in Eastern Europe

9. Constitutional guidelines that make the president the chief foreign-policy maker in the United States do NOT include
   a. being commander in chief.
   b. appointing ambassadors.
   c. appointing justices to the Supreme Court.
   d. negotiating treaties.

10. Which of the following is an ongoing challenge facing today's foreign-policy makers?
    a. Should the Senate ratify SALT II?
    b. How do we balance the U.S. economic and military interests?
    c. Will the U.S. bomb Libya again?
    d. How can we rescue American hostages in Lebanon?

11. The U.S. trade policy with western Europe has resulted in the United States
    a. lowering the price of its exports.
    b. developing a better marketing strategy.
    c. renegotiating its trade agreement.
    d. increasing its trade deficit.

12. In Europe, the United States has been providing one-fourth of the conventional forces and a nuclear arsenal to deter Soviet forces through
    a. NATO.
    b. EEC.
    c. OPEC.
    d. MIRVs.

13. The U.S. trade policy with Japan today allows the Japanese in our markets if they will let us in their markets, emphasizing increased
    a. deficits.
    b. sanctions.
    c. aggression.
    d. reciprocity.

14. Gerald Curtis states that the U.S. military policy with Japan had two objectives: to prevent Japan from being a military power again and to
    a. allow our military forces to be stationed in Japan.
    b. incorporate Japan's fierce warriors into our military.
    c. insure that Japan would be on our side against an adversary.
    d. gain Japan's military bases throughout the Pacific rim.

15. Product "dumping" used by Japan to erect protectionist trade barriers against American-made goods refers to
    a. getting rid of inferior products to reduce losses.
    b. selling below cost to maintain market domination.
    c. putting numerous product samples on the market to determine what the market wants.
    d. sending a new product to a target market.

16. Marvin Kalb states that we are all affected by U.S. foreign policy with western Europe and Japan because
    a. the entire world is hooked into a technological loop.
    b. we all fear a nuclear attack.
    c. so much of our budget is spent on foreign policy.
    d. the U.S. military dominates western Europe and Japan.

Short-Answer Question:
17. Do you believe that the United States should continue to pay large sums of money to maintain the national security of western Europe and Japan while our trade deficit continues to grow? Why or why not?

Answer Key

These are the correct answers with reference to the Learning Objectives, and to the source of the information: the Textbook Focus Points, Schmidt, *et al. American Government and Politics Today* (Schmidt), and the Telelesson Focus Points. Page numbers are also given for the Textbook Focus Points. "KT" indicates questions with Key Terms defined.

Question	Answer	Learning Objective	Textbook Focus Point (page no.)	Telelesson Focus Point
1	A	1	1 (Schmidt, p. 595)............KT	
2	D	1	2 (Schmidt, p. 596)	
3	C	1	3 (Schmidt, p. 598)	
4	C	1	3 (Schmidt, p. 600)	
5	B	2	4 (Schmidt, p. 604)	
6	D	3	5 (Schmidt, p. 605)	
7	C	1	6 (Schmidt, pp. 606-609)	
8	A	1	7 (Schmidt, p. 614)	
9	C	1		1
10	B	1		2
11	D	4		3
12	A	5		4
13	D	4		5
14	C	5		6
15	B	4		7
16	A	6		8

Short Answer:

17		6		8

Lesson 21

The Judiciary

Overview

This lesson and the one on "The Judicial Selection Process" complete our study of the structure of the U.S. government. This lesson focuses on the third branch of government, the judiciary, which—with the executive and legislative branches—forms the three-part system of checks and balances established by the U.S. Constitution. The lessons about the judiciary and the selection process are fundamental to the remaining lessons, about the rights guaranteed by the Constitution that we as Americans enjoy.

Another lesson focuses on how judges are selected. So here we examine the role, structure, and jurisdiction of the federal and state court systems, and find out how cases reach the Supreme Court of the United States. We also analyze how much authority the courts hold in the political process.

Even though the U.S. Constitution established three separate and equal branches of government, in the beginning the judicial branch had to assert itself for equal recognition. It did this with the help of a strong chief justice, John Marshall, and his use of the courts' implied power of judicial review. Some scholars today believe that, through the use of judicial review, the judicial branch has become the most powerful of the three branches.

Except when Supreme Court decisions make headlines, many of us may have little interest in the judiciary. We are apt to view it as just another part of the government, a bunch of stodgy old men in black robes. Not only is that no longer a true description now that women, minorities, and younger people are seated at every level, we also must realize the impact that judicial decisions have on our own lives every day.

Earlier in our study of *Government by Consent* we looked at the historic case of *Brown v. Board of Education of Topeka, Kansas*. Here we examine how this case affected the lives of many people, as well as how it brought up another educational issue: busing. We hear from real people who took the busing issue to the Supreme Court and listen to them tell about their personal experiences and reactions to the Court's decision.

In many ways the judiciary certainly is the least visible and least understood branch of government. But the influence of the judicial branch is profound, and the impact of its decisions often last for many generations.

Learning Objectives

Goal: The purpose of "The Judiciary" is to describe the state and federal court systems, including methods of getting cases to the Supreme Court, how the judiciary influences the political process, and the ways its decisions affect each of us every day.

Objectives:

1. Review the British system upon which most U.S. law is based, including the function of *stare decisis* in the judicial system.

2. Describe the decision-making process of Supreme Court judges, citing precedent and other sources which form the bases for their decisions.

3. Detail the basic structure of the federal and state judicial systems, including the checks placed on the judicial branch.

4. Describe the types of cases that reach the U.S. Supreme Court and the kinds of opinions that form the final decisions.

5. Explain the strategies used by individuals and interest groups to try to influence the judicial system, especially in the case brought by the citizens of Mecklenburg County, North Carolina, in 1965.

6. Show how decisions of the U.S. Supreme Court affect individuals, citing examples from both popular and unpopular court decisions.

7. List the weaknesses of the Supreme Court expressed by Patrick Higgenbotham.

8. Explain judicial review and how it was established.

9. Outline what goes into any judge's decision-making process.

Key Terms

Watch for these terms and pay particular attention to what each one means, as you follow the textbook and telelesson.

Common law	**Opinion**
Precedent	**Majority opinion**
Stare decisis	**Concurring opinion**
Judicial review	**Dissenting opinion**
Original jurisdiction	*Amicus curiae* **briefs**
Trial courts	**Class-action suit**
Jurisdiction	**Political question**
Appellate courts	**Judicial implementation**
Writ of certiorari	

Textbook Reading Assignment

Schmidt, Shelley, and Bardes. *American Government and Politics Today*, 1993-94 edition. Chapter 15, "The Judiciary," pp. 493-508, 520-525.

Textbook Focus Points

Before you read the textbook assignment, review the following points to help focus your thoughts. After you complete the assignment, write out your responses to reinforce what you have learned.

1. On what system is most American law based, and what function does *stare decisis* serve in the American judicial system?

2. What sources other than precedent do the courts consider when making their decisions?

3. What is the basic structure of America's judicial system today?

4. Which cases reach the U.S. Supreme Court, and what types of opinions form the final decisions?

5. How do interest groups participate in the judicial system?

6. What checks are placed on the judicial branch in order to keep our system of government balanced?

Telelesson Interviewees

The following individuals share their expertise in the telelesson:

Reginald Hawkins–Original Plaintiff in *Swann v. Mecklenburg*
Patrick Higgenbotham–Judge, 5th U.S. Circuit Court of Appeals
Arthur R. Miller–Professor, Harvard University Law School
Pauline Paddock–Columnist, *Charlotte Observer*, Charlotte, North
  Carolina
Barefoot Sanders– U.S. District Judge, Northern District of Texas
John R. Schmidhauser–Professor of Political Science, University of
  Southern California

Telelesson Focus Points

Before viewing the telelesson, read over the following points to help
focus your thoughts. After the presentation, write out your responses
to help you remember these important points.

1. Describe the basic structure of the federal courts and the state
   courts.
2. How does the U.S. Supreme Court impact American society, and
   what are some examples that illustrate this?

3. According to Patrick Higgenbotham, what are some weaknesses
   of the Supreme Court?

4. What is judicial review, and how was it established?

5. How did the citizens of Mecklenburg County in Charlotte, North
   Carolina, in 1965 use the courts to accomplish their goals?

6. What influences a judge's decision-making process?

7. Why do people comply with unpopular court decisions?

8. How does Arthur Miller believe the Supreme Court affects the lives of individuals, and why does he call the Supreme Court the "glue" that holds the American enterprise together?

Recommended Reading

The following suggestions are not required unless your instructor assigns them. They are listed to let you know where you can find additional information on areas which interest you.

Abraham, Henry. *The Judicial Process: An Introductory Analysis of the Courts of the United States, England, and France*, 5th edition. New York: Oxford University Press, 1986.

Friedman, Lawrence M. "Judges and Courts: 1850-1900," in *A History of American Law*, 2nd edition. New York: Simon & Schuster, 1985, pp. 371-390.

Harrell, Mary Ann; Burnett Anderson; and the National Geographic Staff. *Equal Justice Under Law: The Supreme Court in American Life*. Washington, D.C.: The Supreme Court Historical Society, 1988.

O'Brien, David M. *Storm Center: Supreme Court in American Politics*. New York: W.W. Norton and Company, 1986.

Tribe, Lawrence. *God Save This Honorable Court*. New York: Random House, 1985.

Getting Involved

These activities are not required unless your instructor assigns them. But they offer good suggestions to help you understand and become more involved in the political process.

1. Note the "Getting Involved" section of your textbook at the end of Chapter 15.
2. Visit a local district court, and write a brief essay evaluating the procedures and organization that you observed.

Self Test

After reading the assignment and watching the telelesson, you should be able to answer these questions. When you have completed the test, turn to the Answer Key to score your answers.

1. Most of American law is based on
   a. Roman law.
   b. English common law.
   c. doctrines of Friedrich Engels.
   d. French civil law.

2. Which of the following is NOT a function of *stare decisis*?
   a. It helps the courts to be more efficient.
   b. It makes a more uniform judicial system.
   c. It makes the law more stable and predictable.
   d. It provides a legal system without bias toward the wealthy.

3. In making decisions, which of the following sources is least likely to be considered by the courts?
   a. Precedent
   b. Constitutions
   c. Public opinion
   d. Statutes

4. The United States has a dual court system of
   a. civil courts and criminal courts.
   b. state courts and federal courts.
   c. misdemeanor courts and felony courts.
   d. state courts and local courts.

5. In the majority of cases it hears, the Supreme Court today rarely acts as a court of original jurisdiction, but rather as
   a. an appellate court.
   b. a trial court.
   c. a criminal court.
   d. a civil court.

6. Interest groups play an important role in our judicial system, because they
   a. can veto judicial nominations.
   b. help to fund the judicial review board.
   c. perform a constitutional duty.
   d. litigate cases.

7. Which of these does NOT serve as a check on the judicial system?
   a. The legislative branch
   b. The executive branch
   c. The general public
   d. The military

8. The major impact of the Supreme Court on American society is through
   a. ruling on civil matters.
   b. decisions on criminal matters.
   c. interpretation of the U.S. Constitution.
   d. judicial review of state constitutions.

9. Patrick Higgenbotham describes the Supreme Court as the least dangerous branch of the U.S. government because
   a. it lacks the power of enforcement.
   b. its members go through the confirmation process.
   c. it depends on Congress to determine its jurisdiction.
   d. the president can alter its philosophical foundation.

10. The Supreme Court asserted its right to reject actions of the executive and legislative branches of government and the lower courts in a concept called
   a. *stare decisis.*
   b. common law.
   c. judicial review.
   d. writ of certiorari.

11. After the parents of a black child filed a lawsuit in 1965 against Mecklenburg County School District to allow their son to attend a predominantly white school near his home, the federal district court judge ordered the school district to
   a. allow the child to attend the location of his choice.
   b. bus 10,000 students for the sole purpose of racial desegregation.
   c. provide transportation to the child's original assignment.
   d. determine how many other black children wanted to attend the white school.

12. According to Barefoot Sanders, judges make their decisions consciously, by following legal precedents, and subconsciously, as a result of the judge's
   a. religious beliefs.
   b. judicial training and political philosophy.
   c. background, experiences, and personal values.
   d. legal experiences and educational background.

13. The issue of school desegregation shows that even after Supreme Court rulings, compliance
    a. cannot be forced.
    b. has to be voluntary.
    c. is carried out by the district courts.
    d. may be slow and painful.

14. Arthur Miller calls the Supreme Court the "glue" that holds the American enterprise together, because it
    a. brokers the fight that develops between Congress and the presidency.
    b. is composed of members who are appointed and not partners in the partisan battle.
    c. has to depend on Congress and the president to implement its decisions.
    d. involves lifetime appointments away from the electoral frenzy.

Short-Answer Question:

15. What role do you believe the federal judiciary should play in the lives of individuals? Why?

Answer Key

These are the correct answers with reference to the Learning Objectives, and to the source of the information: the Textbook Focus Points, Schmidt, *et al. American Government and Politics Today* (Schmidt), and the Telelesson Focus Points. Page numbers are also given for the Textbook Focus Points. "KT" indicates questions with Key Terms defined.

Question	Answer	Learning Objective	Textbook Focus Point (page no.)	Telelesson Focus Point
1.	B	1	1 (Schmidt, p. 495)...........KT	
2.	D	1	1 (Schmidt, pp. 495-496)..KT	
3.	C	2	2 (Schmidt, pp. 496-497)	
4.	B	3	3 (Schmidt, p. 500)	1
5.	A	4	4 (Schmidt, p. 503)...........KT	
6.	D	5	5 (Schmidt, p. 505)	
7.	D	3	6 (Schmidt, p. 520)	
8.	C	6		2
9.	A	7		3
10.	C	8	KT	4
11.	B	5		5
12.	C	9		6
13.	D	6		7
14.	A	6		8

Short Answer:

15.		6	5 (Schmidt, p. 505-508)	2,7,8

York Times

LATE CITY EDITION

Weather: Mostly sunny today; cle
tonight. Mostly sunny tomorro
Temperature range today
yesterday 74-94. Details on page

WEDNESDAY, JULY 8, 1981

30 cents beyond 50-mile zone from New York City.
Higher in air delivery cities.

25 CENT

REAGAN NOMINATING WOMAN, AN ARIZONA APPEALS JUDGE, TO SERVE ON SUPREME COURT

REACTION IS MIXI

Senate Seems Favoral but Opposition Arises on Abortion Stands

By STEVEN R. WEISMAN

Special to The New York Times

WASHINGTON, July 7 — Presid
Reagan announced today that he w
nominate Sandra Day O'Connor, a
year-old judge on the Arizona Cour
Appeals, to the United States
Court. If confirmed, she would bec
the first woman to serve on the Cour

"She is truly a 'person for
seasons,'" Mr. Reagan said this m
ing, "possessing those unique qual
of temperament, fairness, intelloc

Remarks on Court post, page A12

capacity and devotion to the public g
which have characterized the 101 'br
ren' who have preceded her.'"

White House and Justice Departr
officials expressed confidence
Judge O'Connor's views were
ible with those espoused over the y
by Mr. Reagan, who has been b
critical of some past Supreme

The Judicial Selection Process

Overview

Judges have been described as guardians of all the legal rights that the U.S. Constitution guarantees to every citizen. In some judicial decisions, judges have the power to decide between life and death for the accused; in many cases, their rulings set precedent or decide an issue in a way other judges can follow for generations. This lesson describes the characteristics of the people who become judges and explains how they reach that position.

We begin by seeing how judgeships are filled: via election, appointment, or a combination of the two. Judicial experts discuss the advantages and disadvantages of each method of selection.

Although the process for selecting state judges varies from state to state, the election of judges is still popular in many states. But all federal judges are appointed, so we examine that process next, along with the pros and cons of the appointive system. Finally, as we realize that federal judges are appointed for life and that their decisions impact our own lives for generations, we see how imperative it is that only the best qualified people be appointed.

Judicial scholars characterize judges as being activist or restraintist, or as liberal and conservative, because judges bring to the bench their own philosophies, education, and personal experiences. As we examine the appointment of Robert Bork to the Supreme Court, followed by the enormous controversy surrounding the confirmation process, we especially note the reasoning behind Judge Bork's interpretations of the Constitution while he served on the federal circuit court of appeals.

How judges are selected is vitally important, because their decisions have such a far-reaching influence on our lives. Even so, judges are human like the rest of us. The most difficult part of a judge's job is to judge a case on its own merits and not be guided unduly by his or her personal views and philosophies—or even by public outcry. For a judge's overriding goal must be to provide justice for everyone.

Learning Objectives

Goal: The purpose of "The Judicial Selection Process" is to describe the appointive and elective systems of selecting judges, while suggesting ways that individuals can be involved in either procedure.

Objectives:

1. Describe the nomination process for federal judges, as well as the characteristics most likely to be associated with federal and Supreme Court justices.

2. Outline the qualifications required to become a federal judge and how the judicial selection process works, including the importance of the ideology of the candidates and of those who appoint them.

3. Define judicial activism and judicial restraint, and illustrate how these terms apply to the federal judiciary.

4. Explain what judges do while the various courts are in session.

5. Evaluate the two different methods used to select state judges, including some of the problems inherent in each method.

6. List the basic steps for filling a vacancy on the federal bench, and explain the impact of the lifetime term on this process.

7. Describe the opportunities that individuals have to affect the judicial selection process.

Key Terms

Watch for these terms and pay particular attention to what each one means, as you follow the textbook and telelesson.

Senatorial courtesy   **Judicial selection (TV)**
Judicial activism   **Litigious society (TV)**
Judicial restraint

Textbook Reading Assignment

Schmidt, Shelley, and Bardes. *American Government and Politics Today,* 1993-94 edition. Chapter 15, "The Judiciary," pp. 508-520.

Textbook Focus Points

Before you read the textbook assignment, review the following points to help focus your thoughts. After you complete the assignment, write out your responses to reinforce what you have learned.

1. How does the nomination process for federal judges work?

2. What role does ideology play in the judicial selection process?

3. What characteristics are most likely to describe a federal judge or Supreme Court justice?

4. What are the qualifications of federal judges?

5. What are "judicial activism" and "judicial restraint" as these terms apply to the federal judicial system?

Telelesson Interviewees

The following individuals share their expertise in the telelesson:

Anthony Champagne–Professor of Political Economy, University of Texas, Dallas
Arthur R. Miller–Professor, Harvard University Law School
Tom Phillips–Chief Justice, Supreme Court of Texas

Telelesson Focus Points

Before viewing the telelesson, read over the following points to help focus your thoughts. After the presentation, write out your responses to help you remember these important points.

1. What is meant by the term "judicial selection," and why is it important?

2. What do judges do while the various courts are in session?

3. How are state judges selected, and what are some of the problems inherent in the elective method?

4. How long is a federal judge's term of office, and what are the arguments in favor of this type of term?

---

5. What are the basic steps for filling a vacancy on the federal bench?

6. When and how can individuals affect the process of judicial selection?

Recommended Reading

The following suggestions are not required unless your instructor assigns them. They are listed to let you know where you can find additional information on areas which interest you.

Kramer, Michael. "The Brief on Judge Bork." *U.S. News & World Report* 103 (September 14, 1987): pp. 18-24.

Lamar, Jacob V. "Advise and Dissent." *Time* 130 (September 21, 1987): pp. 12-18+.
Press, Aric. "Trying to Leave a Conservative Legacy." *Newsweek* 110 (July 13, 1987): pp. 22-23.

Woodward, Bob, and Scott Armstrong. *The Brethren: Inside the Supreme Court.* New York: Simon and Schuster, 1979.

Getting Involved

These activities are not required unless your instructor assigns them. But they offer good suggestions to help you understand and become more involved in the political process.

1. Select a former or current justice of the U.S. Supreme Court, develop a brief biographical sketch of that justice, and analyze the justice's impact on the Court.

2. Much has been written both criticizing and praising Chief Justice Earl Warren. At one point during his term, there was a movement to impeach him! Research the decisions made by that court, then write a brief essay giving your opinions about Earl Warren and the decisions of that court. Do you think he and his court were too liberal? Should he have been impeached, or was he merely bringing the Supreme Court into the mid-twentieth century?

Self Test

After reading the assignment and watching the telelesson, you should be able to answer these questions. When you have completed the test, turn to the Answer Key to score your answers.

1. Although the president nominates federal judges, the nomination of district court judges typically originates with
   a. the state's governor if from the president's political party.
   b. a senator or senators of the president's party.
   c. members of the House of Representatives from the state where the vacancy occurs.
   d. state bar association in the state where the vacancy occurs.

2. An important factor in the president's choices for the federal judiciary and in the Senate confirmation hearings that follow is the candidate's
   a. occupation.
   b. religion.
   c. age.
   d. ideology.

3. The only relatively predictable characteristic of Supreme Court appointments is that the nominees will be from the same
   a. region of the country as the president.
   b. religious denomination as the president.
   c. age group as the president.
   d. political party as the president.

4. Most federal judges have had experience
   a. as a state judge.
   b. at some level of government.
   c. in an elective office.
   d. teaching in a law school.

5. Judicial scholars like to characterize different Supreme Courts and various Supreme Court justices by how they
   a. view the Constitution and become involved in matters affecting the other branches of government.
   b. write their opinions and how often they are in the majority.
   c. react to public opinion and incorporate it in their decisions.
   d. interact with the other justices and argue their different views.

6. The public's low awareness and lack of involvement in the judicial selection process is a concern because the judiciary
   a. receives large amounts of federal appropriations.
   b. is in session all year.
   c. makes decisions that affect our lives daily.
   d. is confirmed by the House of Representatives.

7. Which one of the following is NOT a judge's responsibility in a court of original jurisdiction?
   a. To determine whether a trial has been conducted properly
   b. To rule on the kinds of evidence that can be introduced
   c. To decide guilt or innocence
   d. To set punishment in a criminal case

8. Which of the following is NOT a method of selecting state judges?
    a. Appointed by the governor with the consent of the legislature
    b. Elected in general elections
    c. Appointed by the House and confirmed by the Senate
    d. Selected by a combination of appointment and election

9. Federal judges are appointed by the president and confirmed by the Senate to serve a
    a. single six-year term.
    b. four-year term, subject to reappointment.
    c. five-year term, eligible to serve a total of twenty years.
    d. lifetime term.

10. When there is a vacancy on a federal district court, the president may select a candidate using the system of
    a. presidential prerogative.
    b. senatorial courtesy.
    c. senatorial privilege.
    d. executive order.

11. Individuals and groups have an opportunity to give their views on a Supreme Court nominee
    a. before the president sends a nomination to the Senate Judiciary Committee.
    b. during the public hearings held by the Senate Judiciary Committee.
    c. before the House of Representatives votes to confirm or reject a nominee.
    d. before the nominee is sworn in before a joint session of Congress.

Short-Answer Question:
12. If you had served on the Senate Judiciary Committee during Robert Bork's hearings, would you have voted to confirm or reject his nomination? Why?

Answer Key

These are the correct answers with reference to the Learning Objectives, and to the source of the information: the Textbook Focus Points, Schmidt, *et al. American Government and Politics Today* (Schmidt), and the Telelesson Focus Points. Page numbers are also given for the Textbook Focus Points. "KT" indicates questions with Key Terms defined.

Question	Answer	Learning Objective	Textbook Focus Point (page no.)	Telelesson Focus Point
1.	B	1	1 (Schmidt, p.509)	
2.	D	2	2 (Schmidt, p.511)	
3.	D	1	3 (Schmidt, p.511)	
4.	B	2	4 (Schmidt, pp.514-515)	
5.	A	3	5 (Schmidt, p.517)	
6.	C	2		1
7.	A	4		2
8.	C	5		3
9.	D	6		4
10.	B	6	1 (Schmidt, p.509)....KT	5
11.	B	7		6

Short Answer:

12.		2		1,5

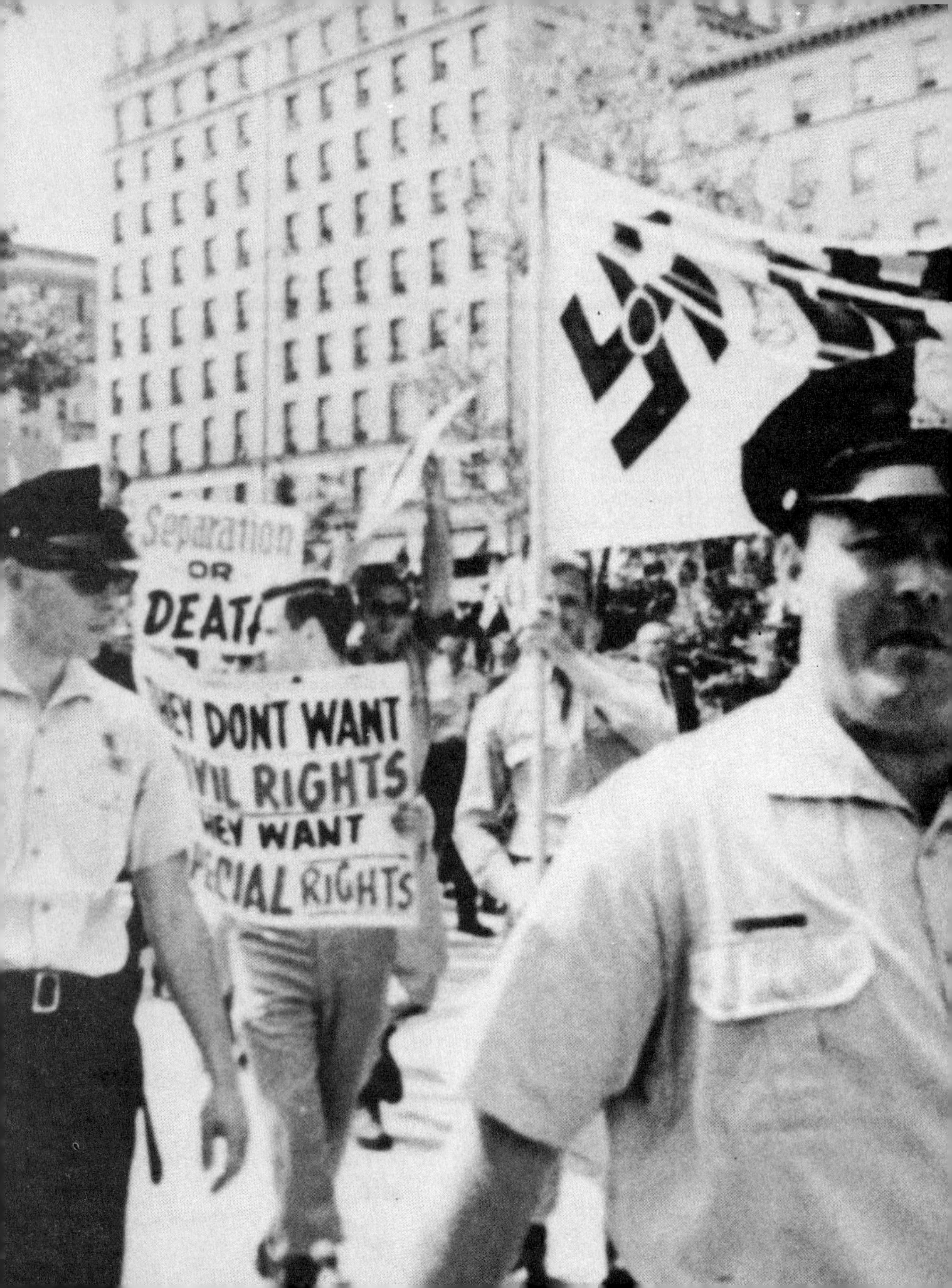
Separation
OR
DONT WANT
RIGHTS
WANT
RIGHTS

Lesson 23

Individual Rights

Overview

This lesson is one of three lessons dealing specifically with the U.S. Bill of Rights. In it we examine why these first ten amendments were proposed and ratified. Then we look at the Fourteenth Amendment and how it has been used to apply most of the Bill of Rights to the states. Finally, we investigate the role of the U.S. Supreme Court in interpreting the Constitution with all of its amendments. Another lesson focuses on the First Amendment freedoms. Yet another lesson highlights the rights guaranteed by the Bill of Rights to a person accused of a crime.

By the time the U.S. Bill of Rights was ratified on December 15, 1791, many states already had their own "bill of rights" in place to protect their citizens from abuse by the state. Therefore, the accepted view was that the national amendments applied only to the national government, a view which the Supreme Court confirmed in 1833 with its decision in *Barron v. Baltimore*.

Thirty-five years later the Fourteenth Amendment placed certain restrictions on the states in order to protect the rights of individuals throughout the nation. But in 1873 the Slaughter-House Cases established dual citizenship, determining that an individual is a citizen both of the nation and of the state in which he or she resides. Then the case of *Gitlow v. New York* began the slow, selective incorporation of the Bill of Rights protection to the states. Several recent and highly emotional cases, dealing with birth control and drug testing, have furthered this incorporation process.

We see how this all works as we talk with people from Skokie, Illinois. They wanted to deny the freedom of speech and assembly to an individual who was an avowed member of the American Nazi Party, while many citizens of Skokie were survivors of concentration camps in Nazi Germany. Cases like these evoke strong emotions; the Supreme Court, in its role as interpreter of the Constitution, must separate public emotion from guaranteed freedoms. The idea that the majority rules is a strong one, and it prevails in the legislative branch. But the courts protect the minority.

Some rights protected by the Bill of Rights are very explicit, where others are more implied. Therefore, we must remember that our rights as individuals are guaranteed by the Constitution *as interpreted* by the Supreme Court of the United States.

Learning Objectives

Goal: The purpose of "Individual Rights" is to demonstrate that the rights of individuals are guaranteed by the U.S. Constitution *as interpreted* by the U.S. Supreme Court.

Objectives:

1. Outline the historical basis for the Bill of Rights, including the people whom it protects and its effect on their daily lives.

2. Explain how the Fourteenth Amendment protects individual rights.

3. Describe how the incorporation theory, especially the "equal protection" and "due process" clauses, affects the application of the Bill of Rights to the states.

4. Illustrate how the Bill of Rights applies to the states with regard to the rights to privacy, gun control, and peaceable assembly.

5. Contrast the roles which constitutional principle and popular emotion play in interpreting the Bill of Rights.

6. Explain the pivotal role of the Supreme Court in balancing individual rights with community rights, using the 1833 Supreme Court decision of *Barron v. Baltimore* as an example.

7. Explain the incident in Skokie, Illinois, as a test of the protection of free speech and right to assemble.

Key Terms

Watch for these terms and pay particular attention to what each one means, as you follow the textbook and telelesson.

Bill of Rights   **Incorporation theory**
Dual citizenship   **Euthanasia**

Textbook Reading Assignment

Schmidt, Shelley, and Bardes. *American Government and Politics Today*, 1993-94 edition. Chapter 4, "Civil Liberties," pp. 103-106, 123-128.

Textbook Focus Points

Before you read the textbook assignment, review the following points to help focus your thoughts. After you complete the assignment, write out your responses to reinforce what you have learned.

1. What is the Bill of Rights, and whom does it protect?

2. How has the Bill of Rights affected your life?

3. How does the Fourteenth Amendment help protect individual rights?

4. What is the incorporation theory, and how has it affected the application of the Bill of Rights to the states?

5. How may states restrict the First Amendment's guarantee of peaceable assembly?

6. On what is the right of privacy based, and to which current issues does it apply?

Telelesson Interviewees

The following individuals will share their expertise in the telelesson:

Erna Gans–Resident of Skokie, Illinois
David Goldberger–Former ACLU Attorney in Skokie, Illinois, Case
Barbara Jordan–Attorney and Professor, LBJ School of Public Affairs, University of Texas, Austin
Lawrence Mann–Attorney for the Railroad Labor Executive Association
Jack Mason–Former Chief Counsel, Federal Railroad Commission
John R. Schmidhauser–Professor of Political Science, University of Southern California
Harvey Schwartz–Former City Attorney for Skokie, Illinois

Telelesson Focus Points

Before viewing the telelesson, read over the following points to help focus your thoughts. After the presentation, write out your responses to help you remember these important points.

1. How are conflicts between constitutional principle and popular emotion resolved?

2. How did the 1833 Supreme Court decision of *Barron v. Baltimore* affect individual rights?

3. How has the Fourteenth Amendment affected individual rights?

4. How does "selective incorporation" relate to the Fourteenth Amendment's "equal protection" and "due process" clauses, and to the Bill of Rights?

5. How have gun-control laws been interpreted in light of the incorporation theory?

6. How did the incident in Skokie, Illinois, test the protection of the rights to free speech and peaceable assembly?

7. How does the Fourth Amendment apply to the right of privacy, and how does this affect drug testing?

Recommended Reading

The following suggestions are not required unless your instructor assigns them. They are listed to let you know where you can find additional information on areas which interest you.

Abraham, Henry J. *Freedom and the Court*. New York: Oxford University Press, 1982.

Hamlin, David. "Swastikas and Survivors: Inside the Skokie Free Speech Case." *The Civil Liberties Review* (March-April 1978).

"The High Cost of Free Speech: ACLU Defense of Nazi Demonstrators in Skokie." *Time* 111 (June 26, 1978): p. 63.

"The High Court Weighs Drug Tests." *Newsweek* 113 (April 3, 1989): p. 8.

Jacoby, Tamar. "Drug Testing on the Dock: Are Safety and Privacy Incompatible?" *Newsweek* 66 (November 14, 1988): p. 66.

Getting Involved

These activities are not required unless your instructor assigns them. But they offer good suggestions to help you understand and become more involved in the political process.

1. Abortion is a very controversial issue, evoking strong emotions from both sides. Set aside your personal beliefs and biases for the moment. Then research the pros and cons for each side, and write a brief essay on what you believe Supreme Court decisions should be on abortion issues and what constitutional basis you use for reaching your decision.

2. Mandatory drug testing is another very emotional issue. Research the topic, then decide which side you support and why. Write a few paragraphs outlining the factors in your decision and how you support your position constitutionally.

Self Test

After reading the assignment and watching the telelesson, you should be able to answer these questions. When you have completed the test, turn to the Answer Key to score your answers.

1. The first ten amendments to the U.S. Constitution, which contain a listing of the rights a person enjoys and which government cannot infringe upon, are called the
   a. writ of habeas corpus.
   b. Bill of Rights.
   c. positive law.
   d. incorporation theory.

2. As originally presented in the Constitution, the Bill of Rights
   a. limited the power of the national, not the state, government.
   b. protected citizens from all forms of government.
   c. protected citizens from both national and state governments.
   d. limited only the power of state governments.

3. It was not until the Fourteenth Amendment was ratified in 1868 that our Constitution explicitly
   a. dealt with the issue of slavery.
   b. addressed civil liberties.
   c. gave blacks the right to vote.
   d. guaranteed everyone due process of the law.

4. The Bill of Rights originally limited only the power of the national government but, through the years, most limitations have been applied to state governments through
   a. the *writ of habeas corpus.*
   b. dual-citizenship rulings.
   c. the selective incorporation theory.
   d. positive law.

---

5. The right of individuals to assemble and protest in public places may be DENIED when
   a. communists are involved.
   b. the Nazi Party is involved.
   c. government opposition is expected.
   d. matters of public safety are at issue.

6. The right to privacy is based on the
   a. concept that all men are created equal.
   b. rights set forth in Article I, Sections 9 and 10.
   c. concept that the Constitution's lack of a specific mention of the right to privacy does not mean that this right is denied.
   d. Twenty-seventh Amendment, which stipulates that all people have certain rights over which the federal government has no authority.

7. Public sentiment is separated from guaranteed freedoms through interpretation of the U.S. Constitution and Bill of Rights by the
   a. president.
   b. Supreme Court.
   c. attorney general.
   d. Congress.

8. The Supreme Court, in deciding *Barron v. Baltimore,*
   a. recognized a dual system of rights.
   b. reinforced the supremacy clause.
   c. made the judicial branch equal with the legislative and executive branches.
   d. initiated the "national commerce" clause.

9. On the basis of the Fourteenth Amendment, the U.S. Supreme Court protected individual rights by placing certain restraints on the
   a. president.
   b. states.
   c. Congress.
   d. bureaucracy.

10. In 1925, the Supreme Court's decision in *Gitlow v. New York* applied the Fourteenth Amendment to
    a. criminal cases.
    b. former slaves.
    c. the states.
    d. the federal government.

11. Some constitutional scholars argue that the Second Amendment does not guarantee an individual the right to bear arms without restriction, because the "right of the people" has been interpreted as a
    a. regional right, for the national militia or armed forces.
    b. state's right, for a state militia or national guard.
    c. collective right, for a group, not individuals.
    d. local right, at the discretion of local governments.

12. The Supreme Court, in deciding the *Skokie* case, was forced to
    a. choose the importance of freedom of speech over freedom to assemble.
    b. defend the statutes of a state government over the statutes of a local government.
    c. divide the issues of popular sentiment from the issues of unpopular sentiment.
    d. separate a constitutional right from a public emotion.

13. Those who oppose mandatory drug testing in the workplace claim that such testing
    a. would infringe on a fundamental constitutional right.
    b. would be a costly process and discriminate against people at lower economic levels.
    c. is an emotional issue that should be left to employers.
    d. is an issue which will police itself and should not be mandatory.

Short-Answer Question:

14. If you had been a judge serving on the court deciding the *Skokie* case, would you have ruled in favor of Frank Collin and the American Nazi Party, or in favor of the citizens of Skokie? On what constitutional point would you have based your decision?

Answer Key

These are the correct answers with reference to the Learning Objectives, and to the source of the information: the Textbook Focus Points, Schmidt, *et al. American Government and Politics Today* (Schmidt), and the Telelesson Focus Points. Page numbers are also given for the Textbook Focus Points. "KT" indicates questions with Key Terms defined.

Question	Answer	Learning Objective	Textbook Focus Point (page no.)	Telelesson Focus Point
1	B	1	1 (Schmidt, p. 103)............KT	
2	A	1	2 (Schmidt, p. 104)............KT	
3	D	2	3 (Schmidt, p. 104)	
4	C	3	4 (Schmidt, p. 105)............KT	
5	D	4	5 (Schmidt, p. 124)	
6	C	4	6 (Schmidt, p. 125)	
7	B	5		1
8	A	6		2
9	B	2		3
10	C	3		4
11	C	4		5
12	D	7		6
13	A	4		7

Short Answer:

14		7	4,5 (Schmidt, p. 123-124)	6

As published by
The New York Times

The Pentagon Papers

The Secret History
of The Vietnam War.

Investigative reporting by Neil Sheehan.
Written by E. W. Kenworthy, Fox Butterfield,
Hedrick Smith and Neil Sheehan.

Lesson 24

First Amendment Freedoms

Overview

This lesson continues the study of the Bill of Rights, focusing solely on the freedoms guaranteed by the First Amendment to the U.S. Constitution. Another lesson covered individual freedoms, many of which are implied. However, the freedoms covered by the First Amendment are very specific: freedom of religion, freedom of speech, freedom of the press, freedom to assemble peaceably, and freedom to petition the government.

But does this specificity mean that these freedoms are absolute? There are those who believe, as did Justice Hugo Black, that the First Amendment freedoms indeed are absolute, because the amendment clearly states that "Congress shall make no law. . . ." Others support the belief that there are shades of gray, or exceptions, to these freedoms, which people could not have known about when it was adopted.

Yet nearly everyone agrees that a democracy cannot exist without the freedoms spelled out in the First Amendment. Hence, the role of the U.S. Supreme Court in interpreting these freedoms, which we studied earlier, grows in significance and difficulty.

We approach our study of the First Amendment freedoms using the doctrine of "preferred position." This says that these freedoms have the highest priority in our constitutional hierarchy, that they are fundamental if democracy as we know it in the United States is to survive. Many constitutional scholars consider the First Amendment more important than the rest of the Bill of Rights or the other amendments to the Constitution.

We also examine conflicts that have arisen between the First Amendment's absolute guarantees and the exceptions, such as freedom of the press versus our right to a public and fair trial, or freedom to worship as we please versus a threat to our safety. In many cases the Supreme Court has applied the "clear and present danger" test in deciding these issues.

As a result, more restrictions have been placed on the freedom to assemble than on any other First Amendment freedom. But these restrictions have been applied to protect an overriding consideration: the public's safety.

Finally, we look at freedom of expression—the basis for the 1989 Supreme Court decision regarding the right to burn the flag. Our review of the cases involving the Pentagon Papers and *Progressive Magazine* can help us better understand other decisions based on this issue.

The democratic form of government is based on our right to speak freely, to organize into groups, to question the decisions and actions of our government, and, if we want, to campaign openly against these. It is imperative that we understand what our First Amendment rights are, for if we do not know what we have to lose, we may forfeit these precious rights guaranteed by the very First Amendment to our Constitution.

Learning Objectives

Goal: The purpose of "First Amendment Freedoms" is to describe the meaning and judicial interpretation of the freedoms guaranteed by the First Amendment and to assess the impact on these rights of individuals.

Objectives:

1. Explain the two principal precepts of freedom of religion as protected by the First Amendment, focusing on the Supreme Court interpretation of the establishment clause and application of the free exercise clause.

2. List restrictions the Supreme Court has placed on the First Amendment guarantee of freedom of expression, including forms of speech that have been unprotected.

3. Review the applications of, and restrictions placed on, the First Amendment guarantee of freedom of the press, including prior restraint, libel, and censorship.

4. Describe the First Amendment guarantee of freedom to assemble peaceably and to petition the government for a redress of grievances, as well as the limitations placed on these freedoms.

5. Outline the First Amendment freedoms and rights, covering general restrictions, who interprets these freedoms, the importance of citizen awareness, and the effect of *Gitlow v. New York* on court decisions.

6. Describe the "clear and present danger" test as it applies to the First Amendment, especially to freedom of religion and freedom of press.

Key Terms

Watch for these terms and pay particular attention to what each one means, as you follow the textbook and telelesson.

Establishment clause	Slander
Free exercise clause	Libel
Clear and present danger test	"Gag" orders
Preferred-position test	Fairness doctrine
Bad-tendency rule	Preferred position doctrine (TV)
Prior restraint	Wall of separation (TV)
Symbolic speech	"Lemon" test (TV)
Commercial speech	Censorship (TV)
Defamation of character	

Textbook Reading Assignment

Schmidt, Shelley, and Bardes. *American Government and Politics Today*, 1993-94 edition. Chapter 4, "Civil Liberties," pp. 106-124.

Textbook Focus Points

Before you read the textbook assignment, review the following points to help focus your thoughts. After you complete the assignment, write out your responses to reinforce what you have learned.

1. What are the two principal precepts of freedom of religion?

2. How has the Supreme Court interpreted the establishment clause of the First Amendment?

3. How has the free exercise clause of the First Amendment been applied?

4. What restrictions have been placed on the First Amendment freedom of expression?

5. What forms of free speech have been unprotected, and how can you determine if certain speech is protected or not?

6. What restrictions have been placed on the First Amendment freedom of the press?

7. What restrictions have been placed on individuals' freedom to assemble and petition their government, as guaranteed by the First Amendment?

Telelesson Interviewees

The following individuals share their expertise in the telelesson:

Jesse Choper–Dean and Professor of Law, University of California Law School, Berkeley

Kenneth Janda–Professor of Political Science, Northwestern University

Brian Landsberg–Professor, McGeorge School of Law, University of the Pacific

John R. Schmidhauser–Professor of Political Science, University of Southern California, Los Angeles

Telelesson Focus Points

Before viewing the telelesson, read over the following points to help focus your thoughts. After the presentation, write out your responses to help you remember these important points.

1. Who restricts or regulates the First Amendment freedoms, and who determines if these restrictions violate the First Amendment?

2. Why is it important for us to know and understand what our First Amendment rights are?

3. What was the significance of *Gitlow v. New York*, and how has this decision affected subsequent court decisions?

4. What is the clear and present danger test, and how has it been applied to freedom of religion?

5. How has the clear and present danger test been applied to freedom of the press?

6. How has the Supreme Court restricted the freedom of assembly, and how critical is this freedom?

7. Why is it important for us to know what our First Amendment freedoms are?

Recommended Reading

The following suggestions are not required unless your instructor assigns them. They are listed to let you know where you can find additional information on areas which interest you.

Drinan, Robert F. "Do Creches Violate the Constitution?" *America* 159 (November 26, 1988): pp. 428-429.

Faulk, John Henry. *Fear on Trial*. New York: Grosset and Dunlap, 1976.

Karlen, Neal. "Busting the Bhagwan." *Newsweek* 106 (November 11, 1985): pp. 26-32.

Orwell, George. *Nineteen Eighty-Four*. San Diego, California: Harcourt, Brace, Jovanovich; 1983.

Sanders, Alain L. "Revisiting the Reindeer Rule." *Time* 132 (December 12, 1988): p. 71.

"Supreme Court Justice Speaks His Mind on Key Issues." *U.S. News & World Report* 65 (December 16, 1968): pp. 55-57.

"Worldly Guru in the Western World." *U.S. News & World Report* 99 (October 14, 1985): p. 15.

Getting Involved

These activities are not required unless your instructor assigns them. But they offer good suggestions to help you understand and become more involved in the political process.

1. In Oregon, a group of religious adherents, the Rajneeshees, literally took over the town of Antelope. They renamed it Rajneeshpuram, instituted their own concept of a religious state, and frightened away many of the former residents. Write a brief essay on how the freedom to believe and practice religion as you please applies to the rights of the Rajneeshees and to the rights of the earlier inhabitants.

2. Research the Supreme Court decision in *Miller v. California*, which established the criteria for judging obscenity. Do you agree with these standards? What changes would you recommend?

Self Test

After reading the assignment and watching the telelesson, you should be able to answer these questions. When you have completed the test, turn to the Answer Key to score your answers.

1. Freedom of religion consists of two principal precepts, the
   a. acknowledgement of God and the right to pray.
   b. freedom to worship and the right of the government to acknowledge the true faith.
   c. power of the government to regulate religion and the right of religious groups to gain political power.
   d. separation of church and state, and the free exercise of religion.

2. In *Lemon v. Kurtzman*, the court ruled that direct state aid might NOT be used to
   a. provide free lunches to church-related schools.
   b. subsidize religious instruction.
   c. purchase Bibles for religious classes.
   d. fund basic education grants to religious colleges.

3. A person can hold any religious belief, or no belief, but the government can become involved and act when
   a. religion advocates the overthrow of the government.
   b. churches try to avoid paying property taxes.
   c. religious practices harm the public welfare.
   d. churches harbor convicted felons.

4. Which of the following is NOT one of the requirements of the obscenity test established in the 1973 *Miller* ruling?
   a. The work violates contemporary community standards.
   b. The work taken as a whole appeals to prurient interest in sex.
   c. The work provokes a community to demonstrate against it.
   d. The work shows patently offensive sexual conduct.

---

5. Libel is
   a. insurance one must have on a motor vehicle.
   b. defamation in writing.
   c. spoken words that cannot be proven.
   d. printed material that is highly controversial.

6. In regard to the right to assemble, municipalities
   a. have to provide an adequate place for all people to meet.
   b. may require permits for demonstrations.
   c. are prohibited from making any restrictions.
   d. have no power to pass limitations without state approval.

7. Any laws restricting or regulating the First Amendment freedoms have their constitutionality decided by the
   a. Supreme Court.
   b. president.
   c. bureaucracies.
   d. Congress.

8. It is vital to understand what rights are guaranteed by the First Amendment, so that we
   a. will know when they are being infringed upon.
   b. can trust our elected officials to guard them.
   c. can have the president uphold the Constitution.
   d. can be informed if we are called to jury duty.

9. The *Gitlow* v. *New York* decision was the first time the Supreme Court said specifically that First Amendment freedoms
   a. can be restricted in any way by the national government.
   b. apply to state and local governments, as well as to the national government.
   c. are secondary in importance to the laws of state governments.
   d. can be interpreted solely by the U.S. Supreme Court.

10. The test used by the Supreme Court to determine if the liberties guaranteed by the First Amendment can be restricted is known as the
    a. positive law test.
    b. bad-tendency rule.
    c. clear and present danger test.
    d. sliding-scale test.

11. In *Engel v. Vitale*, the Court ruled that any prayer written or sanctioned by state officials to further religious beliefs
    a. is permissible if no specific religion is favored.
    b. teaches school children vital life values.
    c. restricts children's religious creativity.
    d. violates the establishment clause of the First Amendment.

12. The cases of the Pentagon Papers and *Progressive Magazine* centered around the action of "prior restraint," also known as
    a. censorship.
    b. espionage.
    c. a "gag" order.
    d. a restraining order.

13. Because no one has the right to deliberately incite others to violence, block traffic, or hold parades just anywhere at any time, the Supreme Court has decided that the power of local authorities to place reasonable restrictions on large public gatherings is
    a. a violation of people's rights to peaceably assemble.
    b. not an infringement on First Amendment liberties.
    c. an example of the national government's supremacy.
    d. a division of power between national and local governments.

14. It is imperative that we understand what our First Amendment rights are, because the First Amendment is the
    a. only amendment with five provisions.
    b. guarantee to hold free elections.
    c. cornerstone of American democracy.
    d. basis of most lawsuits.

Short-Answer Question:

15. Contrast the "absoluteness" versus the "shades of gray" interpretations of First Amendment freedoms, as they relate to your personal beliefs.

Answer Key

These are the correct answers with reference to the Learning Objectives, and to the source of the information: the Textbook Focus Points, Schmidt, *et al. American Government and Politics Today* (Schmidt), and the Telelesson Focus Points. Page numbers are also given for the Textbook Focus Points. "KT" indicates questions with Key Terms defined.

Question	Answer	Learning Objective	Textbook Focus Point (page no.)	Telelesson Focus Point
1	D	1	1 (Schmidt, p. 106)	
2	B	1	1 (Schmidt, p. 110)	
3	C	1	3 (Schmidt, p. 110)	
4	C	2	4 (Schmidt, p. 114)	
5	B	3	5,6 (Schmidt, p. 119)........KT	
6	B	4	7 (Schmidt, p. 123)	
7	A	5		1
8	A	5		2
9	B	5		3
10	C	6	5 (Schmidt, p. 111)..........KT	4
11	D	6	1,2 (Schmidt, pp. 107-108)KT	4
12	A	6	KT	5
13	B	4		6
14	C	5		7

Short Answer:

15		5		7

WARNING TO BE GIVEN BEFORE TAKING
ANY ORAL OR WRITTEN CONFESSION

(1) You have the right to remain silent and not make any statement at all and any statement you make may be used against you at your trial;

(2) Any statement you make may be used as evidence against you in court;

(3) You have the right to have a lawyer present to advise you prior to and during any questioning;

(4) If you are unable to employ a lawyer, you have the right to have a lawyer appointed to advise you prior to and during any questioning; and,

(5) You have the right to terminate the interview at any time.

LEGAL LIAISON DIVISION — DALLAS POLICE DEPARTMENT

POL-81646

Rights of the Accused

Overview

The rights of a society and the rights of a person accused of a crime are always in tension. At the same time, we strongly believe that no innocent person should be punished. This lesson highlights the dynamic conflict between society and the accused, as we continue our study of the Bill of Rights. Here we focus on the procedural rights guaranteed to each of us if we are accused of a crime. As page 120 of the text says, "The emphasis on doing things by the rules, almost without regard to whether the decision itself is fair, is the hallmark of procedural due process."

Society in general supports the idea that the same procedures ought to be followed toward everyone, citizen and non-citizen alike, who is accused of a crime. But we usually don't claim these procedural rights—and we almost never realize how important they are—until or unless we are accused.

We also believe that no government can take away a person's life, liberty, or property without "due process of law," which is why due process is preserved in the Constitution and in Amendments Four through Eight. Some additional points important to our system of justice are the presumption that a person is innocent until proven guilty, and the belief that it is better for the guilty to go free than for one innocent person to be punished unjustly.

To illustrate some of the rights guaranteed in matters of procedure, we examine some landmark Supreme Court decisions:

> *Mapp v. Ohio* (1961) applied the exclusionary rule, which determined what evidence was admissable in court and how it could legally be gathered, favoring the accused.

> *California v. Billy Greenwood* (1988) also applied Amendment Four to the gathering of evidence, but expanded police authority.

> *Gideon v. Wainwright* (1963) extended the Sixth Amendment guarantee of counsel to the states and to poor people.

> *Miranda v. Arizona* (1966) incorporated Amendments Five and Six to guarantee that those accused can have counsel present during interrogation and that the accused have a right to "take the Fifth."

> After *Gideon* and *Miranda* had expanded the rights of the accused, *New York v. Quarles* (1984) restricted these expanded rights by modifying the *Miranda* ruling in the interest of public safety.

The rights of the accused versus the rights of society to be safe and secure in our homes and on our streets is in a constant state of imbalance. But unless all of us can live under the assurance of our constitutional rights, none of us is either truly free or truly protected by the law—or from the law.

Learning Objectives

Goal: The purpose of "Rights of the Accused" is to explain the procedural rights guaranteed by the Bill of Rights that protect individuals accused of a crime and to describe the dynamic conflict between the rights of society and the rights of the accused.

Objectives:

1. Explain how each of these terms relate to the rights of the accused: writ of habeas corpus; due process; trial rights, pretrial rights, and limits on police conduct; the *Miranda* decision, including some exceptions; and the exclusionary rule.

2. Explain the effect of the following landmark cases on the rights of the accused: *Mapp v. Ohio, Gideon v. Wainwright, Miranda v. Arizona,* and *California v. Billy Greenwood.*

3. Assess the conflict in our society over capital punishment, and see how some states have resolved the conflict.

4. Describe the conflict in our society regarding protecting the rights of people accused of a crime versus protecting the rights of everyone else.

5. Show how the Fourth, Fifth, Sixth and Eighth Amendments affect the rights of the accused and protect that person's life, liberty, and property.

Key Terms

Watch for these terms and pay particular attention to what each one means, as you follow the textbook and telelesson.

Writ of habeas corpus	**"Taking the Fifth" (TV)**
Exclusionary rule	*Miranda* **warning (TV)**
Capital crimes (TV)	

Textbook Reading Assignment

Schmidt, Shelley, and Bardes. *American Government and Politics Today*, 1993-94 edition. Chapter 4, "Civil Liberties," pp. 102, 129-138.

Textbook Focus Points

Before you read the textbook assignment, review the following points to help focus your thoughts. After you complete the assignment, write out your responses to reinforce what you have learned.

1. What is a writ of habeas corpus, and how does it protect the rights of the accused?

2. What are some of the basic rights of criminal defendants with regard to trial rights, pre-trial rights, and limits on police conduct?

3. How did the verdict in the *Miranda* decision extend the rights of the accused?

4. What impact have recent Supreme Court rulings had on the *Miranda* decision?

5. What is the exclusionary rule, and how does it protect the rights of the accused?

6. What did Clarence Earl Gideon contribute to the rights of the accused?

7. What is the conflict over capital punishment, and how have some states resolved it?

Telelesson Interviewees

The following individuals share their expertise in the telelesson:

Mary Broderick–National Legal Aid and Defense Association
Reuben Greenberg–Chief of Police, Charleston, South Carolina

Fred Inbau–Professor Emeritus, Northwestern University Law School
Norman Kinne –Assistant District Attorney, Dallas, Texas
Peter Lesser–Criminal Defense Attorney, Dallas, Texas
John R. Schmidhauser–Professor of Political Science, University of Southern California

Telelesson Focus Points

Before viewing the telelesson, read over the following points to help focus your thoughts. After the presentation, write out your responses to help you remember these important points.

1. What conflict arises in our society regarding the rights of the accused, and how are these rights protected?

2. What protection does the Fourth Amendment provide against unreasonable search and seizure?

3. What legal concept did *Mapp v. Ohio* apply, and what effect has this had on the rights of the accused?

4. How did the *Billy Greenwood* case affect the application of the exclusionary rule?

5. How do the provisions of the Eighth Amendment protect the rights of the accused?

6. How does the verdict in the *Gideon* case affect the application of the Sixth Amendment?

7. How does the *Miranda* decision affect the Fifth Amendment provision regarding self-incrimination?

8. What are some exceptions to the *Miranda* ruling?

Recommended Reading

The following suggestions are not required unless your instructor assigns them. They are listed to let you know where you can find additional information on areas which interest you.

Jacoby, Ted. "Fighting Crime by the Rules." *Newsweek* 112 (July 18, 1988): p. 53.

Lewis, Anthony. *Gideon's Trumpet.* New York: Vintage, 1964.

Methvin, Eugene. "The Case of Common Sense vs. Miranda." *Reader's Digest* 131 (August 1987): pp. 96-100.

Sanders, Alain. "Lifting the Lid on Garbage." *Time* 131 (May 30, 1988): p. 54.

"Secrets of Trash." *Fortune* 117 (June 20, 1988): p. 119.

Uviller, H. Richard. " Does It Protect your Garbage?" *Nation* 247 (October 10, 1988): pp. 302-304.

Getting Involved

These activities are not required unless your instructor assigns them. But they offer good suggestions to help you understand and become more involved in the political process.

1. Note the "Getting Involved" section of your textbook at the end of Chapter 4.

2. In order to understand the impact of *Miranda v. Arizona* favoring the accused, talk with a senior or retired police officer and with a junior police officer. Ask them how arrest procedures have changed since the *Miranda* ruling. Do they favor or oppose the decision? Why?

Self Test

After reading the assignment and watching the telelesson, you should be able to answer these questions. When you have completed the test, turn to the Answer Key to score your answers.

1. "You should have the body" is the literal meaning of
   a. Writ of *mandamus*
   b. Writ of *certiorari*
   c. Writ of *habeas corpus*
   d. Exclusionary rule

2. Limits on conduct of police and prosecutors include no
   a. unreasonable or unwarranted searches or seizures.
   b. questioning of individuals until they are arrested.
   c. habeas corpus.
   d. breaking and entering for public safety.

3. In Miranda's appeal, his attorney argued that the police had never informed Miranda that he had the right to
   a. a writ of habeas corpus and the right to reasonable bail.
   b. remain silent and the right to be represented by counsel.
   c. no arrest except for probable cause and the right to appeal conviction.
   d. prompt arraignment and the right to confront all witnesses.

4. The Supreme Court under Chief Justice Warren Burger did not expand the *Miranda* ruling,
   a. but it did change the focus of the ruling.
   b. although it did provide counsel early in questioning.
   c. but instead somewhat reduced its scope and effectiveness.
   d. even though most civil rights groups wanted it to do so.

5. The exclusionary rule prohibits
   a. defendants from testifying in their own behalf.
   b. improperly obtained evidence from being used by prosecutors.
   c. use of evidence seized by means of a search warrant.
   d. defense counsel from having access to legally obtained evidence.

6. The heart of Gideon's petition to the Supreme Court lay in his notion that "to try a poor man for a felony without giving him a lawyer was to deprive him of
   a. the writ of habeas corpus."
   b. taking the Fifth."
   c. his Miranda rights."
   d. due process of law."

7. In 1972, the Supreme Court agreed that the death penalty, as applied in most states, was
   a. random and arbitrary.
   b. rare but fair.
   c. deserved but arbitrary.
   d. a necessary deterrent

8. In determining the guilt or innocence of a defendant, our society accepts the premise that it is better to
   a. follow the principle of "an eye for an eye."
   b. base justice on the code of the West.
   c. allow some guilty persons to go free than for one innocent person to be punished.
   d. punish one innocent person unjustly than for the guilty to escape punishment.

9. The Supreme Court's interpretation of the Fourth Amendment determines if
   a. individuals have been given a fair and legal trial.
   b. evidence has been gathered properly by the police.
   c. individuals have been put in jeopardy twice.
   d. sentences are cruel and unusual punishment.

10. The Supreme Court ruling in *Mapp v. Ohio* that the police had conducted an unreasonable search and seizure was an early application of the legal concept of
    a. writ of habeas corpus.
    b. "taking the Fifth."
    c. the *Miranda* doctrine.
    d. the exclusionary rule.

11. In the *Greenwood* case, the Supreme Court ruled that evidence obtained from the garbage or trash of a criminal suspect without a search warrant is legal because
    a. garbage is considered outside the bounds of an individual's home.
    b. garbage is not of value to anyone.
    c. search warrants can't be specific about the who, where, or why of garbage or trash.
    d. evidence found in a person's garbage can be destroyed easily.

12. The Eighth Amendment comes into play to protect the accused from
    a. unreasonable searches.
    b. double jeopardy.
    c. excessive bail.
    d. self-incrimination.

13. The *Gideon* case concerned the application of the Sixth Amendment
    a. protection from unreasonable searches.
    b. guarantee of right to counsel.
    c. prohibition against excessive bail.
    d. protection from self-incrimination.

14. Which of the following provisions was NOT established in the *Miranda* case?
    a. The accused individual is entitled to an attorney before questioning.
    b. The accused individual must be advised of the constitutional right to remain silent.
    c. Any statement the accused makes may be used against that person.
    d. A defendant cannot be tried for the same crime twice.

15. The *New York v. Quarles* decision modified the *Miranda* ruling, shifting the balance to favor the rights of the
    a. public to be safe and secure, over the rights of the accused.
    b. accused to have a fair trial, over the rights of the public to be safe and secure.
    c. police to prosecute successfully, over the rights of the accused to receive a fair trial.
    d. defendant to have counsel, over the rights of the police to prosecute.

Short-Answer Question:
16. Where do you think the balance of rights is today, in favor of the accused or in favor of society? Why?

Answer Key

These are the correct answers with reference to the Learning Objectives, and to the source of the information: the Textbook Focus Points, Schmidt, *et al. American Government and Politics Today* (Schmidt), and the Telelesson Focus Points. Page numbers are also given for the Textbook Focus Points. "KT" indicates questions with Key Terms defined.

Question	Answer	Learning Objective	Textbook Focus Point (page no.)	Telelesson Focus Point
1	C	1	1 (Schmidt, p. 130)......KT	
2	A	1	2 (Schmidt, p. 129)	
3	B	1	3 (Schmidt, p. 130)	
4	C	2	4 (Schmidt, p. 130)......KT	
5	B	1	5 (Schmidt, p. 132)......KT	
6	D	2	6 (Schmidt, p. 131)	
7	A	3	7 (Schmidt, p. 133)	
8	C	4		1
9	B	5		2
10	D	2	5 (Schmidt, p. 132)......KT	3
11	A	2		4
12	C	5		5
13	B	2,5	6 (Schmidt, p. 131)	6
14	D	5	3 (Schmidt, p. 130)......KT	7
15	A	1	4 (Schmidt, p. 132)	8

Short Answer:

16		4	2 (Schmidt, pp. 132-135)	1

Lesson 26

Women and Minorities

Overview

This lesson completes our study of *Government by Consent,* bringing together concepts and institutional structures we have studied throughout the course. Elsewhere we saw how the Fourteenth Amendment has been used to apply the Bill of Rights to the states through selective incorporation. The "equal protection of the laws" clause of that amendment also serves as the basis for many of the cases filed by women and minority groups. In this lesson, we see how these groups apply this clause in arguing their cases.

Minority groups, especially blacks or African-Americans, have been very successful with the courts; probably the best known and most widely beneficial case is the 1954 decision in Brown v. Board of Education. These groups also have succeeded in having legislation passed to establish and protect their rights as full citizens, such as the 1964 Civil Rights Act, the Voting Rights Act, and the Equal Pay Act.

So far women, however, have not enjoyed the same results, even though they are a majority of the electorate. During the Civil War period many activist women made a conscious decision to push for rights for blacks first, since African-Americans then certainly were in worse straits than women. But it took fifty more years —from 1870 when black men were fully enfranchised, until 1920—for women to simply gain the right to vote. (If you have a grandmother or great-grandmother over age 70 in 1990, she was born without the right to vote if she grew up as a citizen in the United States.)

Working to get the Equal Rights Amendment passed by Congress and presented to the states for ratification took yet another fifty years. Then it was ratified by the majority of state legislatures, but it failed to achieve approval by the required three-fourths of the states and died. This lesson briefly covers what the ERA wanted to achieve, why it failed, and the various ways the ERA and less permanent guarantees of equality for women are being re-introduced in Congress.

The term "equality" often is used synonymously with civil rights: the personal freedoms guaranteed in this country by the Constitution, its amendments, and the laws enacted by Congress. Yet the action toward equality has moved from primarily equal treatment regardless of race, to more equal treatment or equal opportunity for all in the economic and political arenas. This does not overlook the fact that the struggle for racial equality continues; simply that it does so to a lesser degree than the struggle for economic and political equality.

In this lesson we not only examine how and why the civil rights movement in the United States evolved for minority groups and for women, we also assess the current status of civil rights for all. At the same time we examine some of the new problems raised by attempts to solve equality issues.

In short, the struggle for civil rights seems to be perpetual, with only specific issues resolved, one at a time. Equality issues today are broader and more complex than the comparatively simple issue of racial equality; current issues include such concerns as affirmative action, comparable worth, abortion decisions, reverse discrimination, and gay rights. These issues not only involve "balancing acts" similar to those we encounter in criminal justice— trying to be equally fair to both sides—they often come to the forefront based on the so-called "pocketbook issues."

Both minorities and women have come a long way in their fight for equality under the law of the United States of America. The struggle has been neither easy nor static, for the issues and their context change over time. Perhaps the words of Martin Luther King Jr. best sum up the reason why the struggle for legal equality for everyone —with constitutional guarantees—continues: "Injustice anywhere is a threat to justice everywhere."

Learning Objectives

Goal: The purpose of "Women and Minorities" is to describe how women and minorities historically have not enjoyed the same treatment under the law as white males, and to explain how the Fourteenth Amendment, legislation, and judicial interpretation are used to advance the civil rights of all.

Objectives:

1. Describe the types of discrimination against blacks, beginning with their status prior to the Civil War through the nonviolent activities of the 1960s civil rights movement, and how the civil rights legislation it produced has affected American society since then.

2. Explain in what ways the difficulty that Hispanics (Latinos) have had, in entering the political mainstream and achieving power, differ from the problems faced by African-Americans.

3. Describe how the legal status of the American Indian differs from that of other minorities and women, as well as what the U.S. government has done to address the unique problems of these Native Americans.

4. Contrast the types of discrimination toward Asian-Americans in the past with that experienced today.

5. Outline the struggle for equality for all people, including the revised concept of the "melting pot" and projections of new issues in civil rights.

6. Highlight the various forms of discrimination against women, beginning with women's struggle to gain suffrage and continuing through current efforts to make them equal citizens in every respect, then highlight the effects of legislation and judicial decisions on their progress.

7. List the major problems facing the elderly today, along with what attempts are being made to alleviate these problems.

8. Review actions taken to increase public awareness and protect the rights of handicapped individuals, as well as how such action benefits the rest of society.

9. Describe the rights of juveniles, considering the low status in which they are seemingly held.

10. Outline the rights of the gay population and the roles organized groups are playing in American politics.

11. Analyze the impact of the black civil rights movement on other groups that were not, or still may not be, receiving equal treatment under the law.

Key Terms

Watch for these terms and pay particular attention to what each one means, as you follow the textbook and telelesson.

"Separate but equal" doctrine
De facto segregation
De jure segregation
Busing
Equal Employment Opportunity
  Commission
Affirmative action

Reverse discrimination
White primary
Poll tax
Suffrage
Sex discrimination
Sexual harassment
Comparable worth

Textbook Reading Assignment

Schmidt, Shelley, and Bardes. *American Government and Politics Today*, 1993-94 edition. Chapter 5, "Minority Rights," pp. 139-176, and Chapter 6, "Striving for Equality," pp.177-206.

Textbook Focus Points

Before you read the textbook assignment, review the following points to help focus your thoughts. After you complete the assignment, write out your responses to reinforce what you have learned.

1. Outline the legal status of blacks prior to the Civil War, and from then until the 1960s civil rights movement.

2. Describe the nonviolent activities of the 1960s civil rights movement.

3. Explain the major civil rights legislation of the 1960s and its effect on American society.

4. If the Fifteenth Amendment gave everyone, except women, the right to vote, why was the Voting Rights Act of 1965 necessary, and what did the act provide?

5. Why have Hispanics had difficulty achieving political power, and what attempts have they made to enter the political mainstream?

6. How do Native Americans differ from other minorities and women in legal terms, and what has the government done to address this situation?

7. How and why have Asian-Americans experienced discrimination at various times in U.S. history, including today?

8. How is the "melting pot" idea being revised now?

9. Describe the struggle of women in the United States to gain "suffrage," the right to vote.

10. What are some of the major arenas in which women are still struggling to achieve equal status?

11. How has the federal government responded to different types of sex discrimination in jobs?

12. What are the major problems of elderly people today, and what are they doing to try to alleviate these problems?

13. What actions have handicapped individuals taken to bring their needs to the public's attention, and what actions has the government taken to protect their rights?

14. What rights do juveniles have, and why is their status so low?

15. What rights do gays have, and what role are they playing in American politics?

Telelesson Interviewees

The following individuals share their expertise in the telelesson:

Richard L. Dockery–Member of the Clergy; Southwest Regional Director, National Association for the Advancement of Colored People

Andy Hernandez–President, Southwest Voter Registration Education Project

Eleanor Holmes Norton–Professor, Georgetown University Law School

Barbara Jordan–Attorney and Professor, LBJ School of Public Affairs, University of Texas, Austin

Randall Kennedy–Professor, Harvard University Law School

Sarah Weddington–Attorney; Associate Professor of Government and American Studies, University of Texas, Austin

Telelesson Focus Points

Before viewing the telelesson, read over the following points to help focus your thoughts. After the presentation, write out your responses to help you remember these important points.

1. Why is the struggle for equality so difficult?

2. How did the black civil rights movement affect later efforts by other minority groups?

3. How have blacks struggled to gain their civil rights, and what are some of the remedies prescribed to resolve this situation?

4. How were women "protected" by laws, even after they were guaranteed the right to vote?

5. What have women done to raise themselves above "second class" status?

6. Why has it been difficult for Hispanics to gain civil rights?

7. According to Randall Kennedy, what new civil rights issues will we be facing?

Recommended Reading

The following suggestions are not required unless your instructor assigns them. They are listed to let you know where you can find additional information on areas which interest you.

Blow, Richard. "Those Were the Gays." *New Republic* 197 (November 2, 1987): pp. 14-16+.

Brown, Dee. *Bury My Heart at Wounded Knee*. New York: Holt, Rinehart and Winston, 1971.

Davidson, Bill. "Our Largest Minority: Americans with Handicaps." *McCalls* 114 (September 1987): pp. 61-68.

Friedan, Betty. *The Feminine Mystique*. New York: W.W. Norton, 1963.

Gibbs, Nancy R. "Grays on the Go." *Time* 131 (February 22, 1988): pp. 66-70+.

Griffin, John H. *Black Like Me*. Boston: Houghton Mifflin Co., 1977.

King, Martin Luther, Jr. "Letter from the Birmingham Jail." In *A Testament of Hope*, edited by James Melvin Washington. San Francisco: Harper & Row, 1986. [Reprinted with permission at the end of this Study Guide.]

Mansbridge, Jane J. *Why We Lost the E.R.A.* Chicago: University of Chicago Press, 1986.

McCormick, John. "America's Third World." *Newsweek* 112 (August 8, 1988): pp. 20-24+.

Meyer, Dylan S. *Uprooted American: The Japanese-American and the War Relocation Authority During World War II.* Tucson: University of Arizona Press, 1971.

Ramirez, Anthony. "America's Super Minority." *Fortune* 114 (November 24, 1986): pp. 148-149+.

Whitman, David. "For Latinos, A Growing Divide." *U.S. News & World Report* 103 (August 10, 1987): pp. 47-49.

Getting Involved

These activities are not required unless your instructor assigns them. But they offer good suggestions to help you understand and become more involved in the political process.

1. Note the "Getting Involved" sections in your textbook at the end of Chapters 5 and 6.

2. Participate in a Handicapped Awareness Week, so that you can become more aware of the problems that a handicapped person frequently encounters and the need for additional legislative protection.

Self Test

After reading the assignment and watching the telelesson, you should be able to answer these questions. When you have completed the test, turn to the Answer Key to score your answers.

1. Prior to any amendments to the United States Constitution, slaves were
   a. illegal because of the language of Article I.
   b. to be freed after twenty-five years except in the southern states.
   c. referred to as "other persons."
   d. essential for a free-market economy.

2. The Supreme Court invalidated the 1875 Civil Rights Act because the Fourteenth Amendment was
   a. held to be unconstitutional.
   b. depriving minorities of their basic rights.
   c. an attempt to end discrimination by allowing reverse discrimination.
   d. aimed at limiting state action, not actions of private citizens.

3. In the case of *Brown v. Board of Education* (1954), the Supreme Court held that
   a. ethnic minorities have no right to equal treatment by the government.
   b. public-school segregation of races violates the equal protection clause of the Fourteenth Amendment.
   c. the national government does not have the power to force any type of action on local school boards.
   d. the separation of races for a reason like education is not a violation of the Constitution.

4. The civil rights movement led by Martin Luther King Jr. was based on the philosophy of
   a. nonviolent civil disobedience.
   b. divide and conquer.
   c. "equality for all, through strong force when necessary."
   d. equality of practice that did not have to exclude racial segregation.

5. The Civil Rights Acts of 1964 and 1968 and the Voting Rights Act of 1965 marked the resumption by Congress of a leading role in
   a. deciding domestic policies rather than leaving them to the president.
   b. becoming involved in interstate commerce as it affects the national trade policy.
   c. enforcing the constitutional idea of equality for all Americans.
   d. lawmaking, rather than reacting to the proposals of the president and bureaucratic agencies.

6. Title VII of the Civil Rights Act of 1964 forms the cornerstone of employment-discrimination law, because it prohibits discrimination in employment based on
   a. abusive child-labor laws.
   b. race, color, religion, sex, or national origin.
   c. description and responsibilities of the job.
   d. membership in labor unions.

7. One of the major provisions of the Voting Rights Act of 1965 was to
   a. eliminate discriminatory voter-registration tests.
   b. give members of all races the opportunity to vote.
   c. let state governments make all decisions about voting requirements.
   d. end the preponderance of males holding public office.

8. Even though Hispanics represent over 8 percent of the American population, they have had difficulty achieving political power, particularly at the national level, because they have
   a. few strong leaders and low voter turnout.
   b. placed little emphasis on education.
   c. problems finding employment and speaking English.
   d. great national diversity and geographical dispersion.

9. A major distinction between American Indians and other ethnic minorities is that Native Americans were
   a. never discriminated against.
   b. designated by Congress to be citizens of foreign nations.
   c. not given rights that are protected by the Constitution.
   d. not qualified to become citizens for religious reasons.

10. Asian Americans typically are not thought of as being discriminated against because they
    a. are a very new group in the United States.
    b. have considerable representation in Congress.
    c. do not attempt to resist racial discrimination.
    d. earn a relatively high median income.

11. The revision of the "melting pot" idea is happening due to a new emphasis on
    a. excluding groups that are not willing to accept traditional American values.
    b. legislation that would restrict the number of immigrants to the United States.
    c. majority rights as opposed to minority rights.
    d. ethnic and racial pride.

12. The first political cause in which women as a group became active was the
    a. abolition movement.
    b. right to vote.
    c. right to own property without masculine approval.
    d. equal rights movement.

13. The representation of women in political office
    a. is considerably less today than it was in the first years after the Nineteenth Amendment.
    b. exceeds the percentage of voters who are women.
    c. is higher in the United States than in any other country.
    d. does not reflect the participation of women as voters.

14. The prospects for ratification of an Equal Rights Amendment may be
    a. uncertain, but the National Organization for Women and related groups, however, continue the struggle.
    b. slim, because a majority of Americans are opposed to such action.
    c. finished for this century, because a rejected amendment cannot be re-submitted for fifty years.
    d. very poor, because most women now think that such an amendment would greatly hurt their social position.

15. With reference to women's rights, protective legislation is legislation
    a. that prohibits women from becoming military officers.
    b. that protects a woman's inheritance from her husband.
    c. that seeks to protect the health and morals of women.
    d. that prohibits women from taking jobs deemed too dangerous or strenuous.

16. A major change in society's attitude toward age today stems from the growing number of
    a. births, compared to the "baby boom" era.
    b. people age 65 or over.
    c. teenagers.
    d. elderly not reaching their predicted life expectancy.

17. Congress passed the Rehabilitation Act in 1973, which prohibited discrimination against people with a handicap
    a. by prohibiting any reference to a handicap on job applications.
    b. by providing job training and placement programs.
    c. in programs receiving federal aid.
    d. in areas of employment where a handicap was not a factor.

18. The largest group of individuals in the United States with the smallest amount of rights and protection are
    a. women.
    b. Mexican-Americans.
    c. the elderly.
    d. children.

19. The rights and status of homosexuals was ruled upon by the Supreme Court in a case from the state of Georgia in 1986, in which the court held that
    a. state governments cannot discriminate against "gay" sexual conduct.
    b. engaging in homosexual sodomy is not a fundamental right.
    c. people have a fundamental right to practice sexual conduct without government interference.
    d. sexual conduct is a state concern over which the Supreme Court has no jurisdiction.

20. In one sense, the battle for full equality can never be over because
    a. equality is an ideal that can never be achieved.
    b. minority groups do not know how to achieve full equality.
    c. the goals of many minorities change as they progress up the equality ladder.
    d. minorities are never satisfied with their achievements.

21. The black civil rights movement paved the way for later efforts by other minority groups by
    a. using legislation instead of the courts.
    b. using violence as a method of demonstration.
    c. giving them hope that they too might succeed.
    d. dividing minorities in establishing a common goal.

22. In 1896 in *Plessy v. Ferguson*, the Supreme Court ruled that blacks could not be denied equality, but said the
    a. threat of a clear and present danger existed.
    b. no pain/no gain doctrine was applicable.
    c. heterogeneous segregation doctrine was exemplified.
    d. separate and equal concept was acceptable.

23. Which of the following was NOT used as a basis for denying women their civil rights in order to "protect" them?
    a. Running for political office would expose them to vulgarity and sinful vices.
    b. The paternalistic system labeled them weaker and more fragile than men.
    c. Politics would destroy their femininity and harden their personal values.
    d. They would have to meet the same requirements as their male counterparts.

24. Which of the following ways is the only one that does NOT show that women were gaining political power during the 1972 presidential campaign?
    a. A woman was named chair of a national party.
    b. A record number of women were convention delegates.
    c. More women than men voted.
    d. Political campaigns were staffed primarily by women volunteers.

25. Hispanics, the second-largest ethnic minority group in the United States, often face the additional challenge of
    a. a question of identity.
    b. a void of leadership.
    c. a language barrier.
    d. an economic drought.

26. Randall Kennedy states that, in the past, we have thought of the race question as a black/white issue, but the race issue of the future will be part of the larger issue of
    a. politics.
    b. difference.
    c. age.
    d. economics.

Short-Answer Questions:
27. Do you believe that American society has become a "melting pot" or an "ethnic stew"? Why?

28. In terms of discrimination, explain Martin Luther King Jr.'s statement: "Injustice anywhere is a threat to justice everywhere."

Answer Key

These are the correct answers with reference to the Learning Objectives, and to the source of the information: the Textbook Focus Points, Schmidt, *et al. American Government and Politics Today* (Schmidt), and the Telelesson Focus Points. Page numbers are also given for the Textbook Focus Points. "KT" indicates questions with Key Terms defined.

Question	Answer	Learning Objective	Textbook Focus Point (page no.)	Telelesson Focus Point
1	C	1	1 (Schmidt, p. 142)	
2	D	1	1 (Schmidt, p. 144)	
3	B	1	1 (Schmidt, p. 145)	
4	A	1	2 (Schmidt, p. 149)	
5	C	1	3 (Schmidt, p. 153)	
6	B	1	3 (Schmidt, p. 154)	
7	A	1	4 (Schmidt, p. 159)	
8	D	2	5 (Schmidt, p. 161)	
9	B	3	6 (Schmidt, p. 166)	
10	D	4	7 (Schmidt, p. 168)	
11	D	5	8 (Schmidt, p. 170)	
12	A	6	9 (Schmidt, p. 179)	
13	D	6	10 (Schmidt, p. 181)	
14	A	6	10 (Schmidt, p. 185)	
15	D	6	11 (Schmidt, p. 185)	
16	B	7	12 (Schmidt, p. 191)	
17	C	8	13 (Schmidt, p. 195)	
18	D	9	14 (Schmidt, p. 198)	
19	B	10	15 (Schmidt, p. 202)	
20	A	5		1
21	C	11		2
22	D	1		KT...3
23	D	6		4
24	A	6		5
25	C	2		6
26	B	5		7

Short Answer:

27		5	8 (Schmidt, p. 169-171)	
28		11		1

Letter From Birmingham City Jail

by Martin Luther King, Jr.

Dr. King wrote this famous essay (written in the form of an open letter) on 16 April 1963 while in jail. He was serving a sentence for participating in civil rights demonstrations in Birmingham, Alabama. He rarely took time to defend himself against his opponents. But eight prominent "liberal" Alabama clergymen, all white, published an open letter earlier in January that called on King to allow the battle for integration to continue in the local and federal courts, and warned that King's nonviolent resistance would have the effect of inciting civil disturbances. Dr. King wanted Christian ministers to see that the meaning of Christian discipleship was at the heart of the African American struggle for freedom, justice, and equality.

My Dear Fellow Clergymen,

While confined here in the Birmingham city jail, I came across your recent statement calling our present activities "unwise and untimely." Seldom, if ever, do I pause to answer criticism of my work and ideas. If I sought to answer all of the criticisms that cross my desk, my secretaries would be engaged in little else in the course of the day, and I would have no time for constructive work. But since I feel that you are men of genuine good will and your criticisms are sincerely set forth, I would like to answer your statement in what I hope will be patient and reasonable terms.

I think I should give the reason for my being in Birmingham, since you have been influenced by the argument of "outsiders coming in." I have the honor of serving as president of the Southern Christian Leadership Conference, an organization operating in every southern state, with headquarters in Atlanta, Georgia. We have some eighty-five affiliate organizations all across the South—one being the Alabama Christian Movement for Human Rights. Whenever necessary and possible we share staff, educational and financial resources with our affiliates. Several months ago our local affiliate here in Birmingham invited us to be on call to engage in a nonviolent direct-action program if such were deemed necessary. We readily consented and when the hour came we lived up to our promises. So I am here, along with several members of my staff, because we were invited here. I am here because I have basic organizational ties here.

Beyond this, I am in Birmingham because injustice is here. Just as the eighth century prophets left their little villages and carried their "thus sayith the Lord" far beyond the boundaries of their hometowns; and just as the Apostle Paul left his little Tarsus and carried the gospel of Jesus Christ to practically every hamlet and city of the Graeco-Roman world, I too am compelled to carry the gospel of reedom beyond my particular hometown. Like Paul, I must constantly respond to the Macedonian call for aid.

Moreover, I am cognizant of the interrelatedness of all communities and states. I cannot sit idly by in Atlanta and not be concerned about what happens in Birmingham. Injustice anywhere is a threat to justice everywhere. We are caught in an inescapable network of mutuality, tied in a single garment of destiny. Whatever affects one directly affects all indirectly. Never again can we afford to live with the narrow, provincial "outside agitator" idea. Anyone who lives in the United States can never be considered an outsider anywhere in this country.

You deplore the demonstrations that are presently taking place in Birmingham. But I am sorry that your statement did not express a similar concern for the conditions that brought the demonstrations into being. I am sure that each of you would want to go beyond the superficial social analyst who looks merely at effects, and does not grapple with underlying causes. I would not hesitate to say that it is unfortunate that so-called demonstrations are taking place in Birmingham at this time, but I would say in more emphatic terms that it is even more unfortunate that the white power structure of this city left the Negro community with no other alternative.

In any nonviolent campaign there are four basic steps: (1) collection of the facts to determine whether injustices are alive, (2) negotiation, (3) self-purification, and (4) direct action. We have gone through all of these steps in Birmingham. There can be no gainsaying of the fact that racial injustice engulfs this community.

Birmingham is probably the most thoroughly segregated city in the United States. Its ugly record of police brutality is known in every section of this country. Its injust treatment of Negroes in the courts is a notorious reality. There have been more unsolved bombings of Negro homes and churches in Birmingham than any city in this nation. These are the hard, brutal and unbelievable facts. On the basis of these conditions Negro leaders sought to negotiate with the city fathers. But the political leaders consistently refused to engage in good faith negotiation.

Then came the opportunity last September to talk with some of the leaders of the economic community. In these negotiating sessions certain promises were made by the merchants—such as the promise to remove the humiliating racial signs from the stores. On the basis of these promises Rev. Shuttlesworth and the leaders of the Alabama Christian Movement for Human Rights agreed to call a moratorium on any type of demonstrations. As the weeks and months unfolded we realized that we were the victims of a broken promise. The signs remained. Like so many experiences of the past we were confronted with blasted hopes, and the dark shadow of a deep disappointment settled upon us. So we had no alternative except that of preparing for direct action, whereby we would present our very bodies as a means of laying our case before the conscience of the local and national community. We were not unmindful of the difficulties involved. So we decided to go through a process of self-purification. We started having workshops on nonviolence and repeatedly asked ourselves the questions, "Are you able to accept blows without retaliating?" "Are you able to endure the ordeals of jail?" We decided to set our direct-action program around the Easter season, realizing that with the exception of Christmas, this was the largest shopping period of the year. Knowing that a strong economic withdrawal program would be the by-product of direct action, we felt that this was the best time to bring pressure on the merchants for the needed changes. Then it occurred to us that the March election was ahead and so we speedily decided to postpone action until after election day. When we discovered that Mr. Connor was in the run-off, we decided again to postpone action so that the demonstrations could not be used to cloud the issues. At this time we agreed to begin our nonviolent witness the day after the run-off.

This reveals that we did not move irresponsibly into direct action. We too wanted to see Mr. Connor defeated; so we went through postponement after postponement to aid in this community need. After this we felt that direct action could be delayed no longer.

You may well ask, "Why direct action? Why sit-ins, marches, etc.? Isn't negotiation a better path?" You are exactly right in your call for negotiation. Indeed, this is the purpose of direct action. Nonviolent direct action seeks to create such a crisis and establish such creative tension that a community that has constantly refused to negotiate is forced to confront the issue. It seeks so to dramatize the issue that it can no longer be ignored. I just referred to the creation of tension as a part of the work of the nonviolent resister. This may sound rather shocking. But I must confess that I am not afraid of the word tension. I have earnestly worked and preached against violent tension, but there is a type of constructive nonviolent tension that is necessary for growth. Just as Socrates felt that it was necessary to create a tension in the mind so that individuals could rise from the bondage of myths and half-truths to the unfettered realm of creative analysis and objective appraisal, we must see the need of having nonviolent gadflies to create the kind of tension in society that will help men to rise from the dark depths of prejudice and racism to the majestic heights of understanding and brotherhood. So the purpose of the direct action is to create a situation so crisis-packed that it will inevitably open the door to negotiation. We, therefore, concur with you in your call for negotiation. Too long has our beloved Southland been bogged down in the tragic attempt to live in monologue rather than dialogue.

One of the basic points in your statement is that our acts are untimely. Some have asked, "Why didn't you give the new administration time to act?" The only answer that I can give to this inquiry is that the new administration must be prodded about as much as the outgoing one before it acts. We will be sadly mistaken if we feel that the election of Mr. Boutwell will bring the millennium to Birmingham. While Mr. Boutwell is much more articulate and gentle than Mr. Connor, they are both segregationists, dedicated to the task of maintaining the status quo. The hope I see in Mr. Boutwell is that he will be reasonable enough to see the futility of massive resistance to desegregation. But he will not see this without pressure from the devotees of civil rights. My friends, I must say to you that we have not made a single gain in civil rights without determined legal and nonviolent pressure. History is the long and tragic story of the fact that privileged groups seldom give up their privileges voluntarily. Individuals may see the moral light and voluntarily give up their unjust posture; but as Reinhold Niebuhr has reminded us, groups are more immoral than individuals.

We know through painful experience that freedom is never voluntarily given by the oppressor; it must be demanded by the oppressed. Frankly, I have never yet engaged in a direct action movement that was "well-timed," according to the timetable of those who have not suffered unduly from the disease of segregation. For years now I have heard the words "Wait!" It rings in the ear of every Negro with a piercing familiarity. This "Wait" has almost always meant "Never." It has been a tranquilizing thalidomide, relieving the emotional stress for a moment, only to give birth to an ill-formed infant of frustration. We must come to see with the distinguished jurist of yesterday that "justice too long delayed is justice denied." We have waited for more than 340 years for our constitutional and God-given rights. The nations of Asia and Africa are moving with jetlike speed toward the goal of political independence, and we still creep at horse and buggy pace toward the gaining of a cup of coffee at a lunch counter. I guess it is easy for those who have never felt the stinging darts of segregation to say, "Wait." But when you have seen vicious mobs lynch your mothers and fathers at will and drown your sisters and brothers at whim; when you have seen hate-filled policemen curse, kick, brutalize and even kill your black brothers and sisters with impunity; when you see the vast majority of your twenty million Negro brothers smothering in an airtight cage of poverty in the midst of an affluent society; when you suddenly find your tongue twisted and your speech stammering as you seek to explain to your six-year-old daughter why she can't go to the public amusement park that has just been advertised on television, and see tears welling up in her little eyes when she is told that Funtown is closed to colored children, and see the depressing clouds of inferiority begin to form in her little mental sky, and see her begin to distort her little personality by unconsciously developing a bitterness toward white people; when you have to concoct an answer for a five-year-old son asking in agonizing pathos:

"Daddy, why do white people treat colored people so mean?"; when you take a cross-country drive and find it necessary to sleep night after night in the uncomfortable corners of your automobile because no motel will accept you; when you are humiliated day in and day out by nagging signs reading "white" and "colored"; when your first name becomes "nigger" and your middle name becomes "boy" (however old you are) and your last name becomes "John," and when your wife and mother are never given the respected title "Mrs."; when you are harried by day and haunted by night by the fact that you are a Negro, living constantly at tiptoe stance never quite knowing what to expect next, and plagued with inner fears and outer resentments; when you are forever fighting a degenerating sense of "nobodiness"; then you will understand why we find it difficult to wait. There comes a time when the cup of endurance runs over, and men are no longer willing to be plunged into an abyss of injustice where they experience the blackness of corroding despair. I hope, sirs, you can understand our legitimate and unavoidable impatience.

You express a great deal of anxiety over our willingness to break laws. This is certainly a legitimate concern. Since we so diligently urge people to obey the Supreme Court's decision of 1954 outlawing segregation in the public schools, it is rather strange and paradoxical to find us consciously breaking laws. One may well ask, "How can you advocate breaking some laws and obeying others?" The answer is found in the fact that there are two types of laws: there are *just* and there are *unjust* laws. I would agree with Saint Augustine that "An unjust law is no law at all."Now what is the difference between the two? How does one determine when a law is just or unjust? A just law is a man-made code that squares with the moral law or the law of God. An unjust law is a code that is out of harmony with the moral law. To put it in the terms of Saint Thomas Aquinas, an unjust law is a human law that is not rooted in eternal and natural law. Any law that uplifts human personality is just. Any law that degrades human personality is unjust. All segregation statutes are unjust because segregation distorts the soul and damages the personality. It gives the segregator a false sense of superiority, and the segregated a false sense of inferiority. To use the words of Martin Buber, the great Jewish philosopher, segregation substitutes an "I-it" relationship for the "I-thou" relationship, and ends up relegating persons to the status of things. So segregation is not only politically, economically and sociologically unsound, but it is morally wrong and sinful. Paul Tillich has said that sin is separation. Isn't segregation an existential expression of man's tragic separation, an expression of his awful estrangement, his terrible sinfulness? So I can urge men to disobey segregation ordinances because they are morally wrong.

Let us turn to a more concrete example of just and unjust laws. An unjust law is a code that a majority inflicts on a minority that is not binding on itself. This is difference made legal. On the other hand a just law is a code that a majority compels a minority to follow that it is willing to follow itself. This is sameness made legal.

Let me give another explanation. An unjust law is a code inflicted upon a minority which that minority had no part in enacting or creating because they did not have the unhampered right to vote. Who can say that the legislature of Alabama which set up the segregation laws was democratically elected? Throughout the state of Alabama all types of conniving methods are used to prevent Negroes from becoming registered voters and there are some counties without a single Negro registered to vote despite the fact that the Negro constitutes a majority of the population. Can any law set up in such a state be considered democratically structured?

These are just a few examples of unjust and just laws. There are some instances when a law is just on its face and unjust in its application. For instance, I was arrested Friday on a charge of parading without a permit. Now there is nothing wrong with an ordinance which requires a permit for a parade, but when the ordinance is used to preserve segregation and to deny citizens the First Amendment privilege of peaceful assembly and peaceful protest, then it becomes unjust.

I hope you can see the distinction I am trying to point out. In no sense do I advocate evading or defying the law as the rabid segregationist would do. This would lead to anarchy. One who breaks an unjust law must do it *openly, lovingly* (not hatefully as the white mothers did in New Orleans when they were seen on television screaming, "nigger, nigger, nigger"), and with a willingness to accept the penalty. I submit that an individual who breaks a law that conscience tells him is unjust, and willingly accepts the penalty by staying in jail to arouse the conscience of the community over its injustice, is in reality expressing the very highest respect for the law.

Of course, there is nothing new about this kind of civil disobedience. It was seen sublimely in the refusal of Shadrach, Meshach, and Abednego to obey the laws of Nebuchadnezzar because a higher moral law was involved. It was practiced superbly by the early Christians who were willing to face hungry lions and the excruciating pain of chopping blocks, before submitting to certain unjust laws of the Roman Empire. To a degree academic freedom is a reality today because Socrates practiced civil disobedience.

We can never forget that everything Hitler did in Germany was "legal" and everything the Hungarian freedom fighters did in Hungary was "illegal." It was "illegal" to aid and comfort a Jew in Hitler's Germany. But I am sure that if I had lived in Germany during that time I would have aided and comforted my Jewish brothers even though it was illegal. If I lived in a Communist country today where certain principles dear to the Christian faith are suppressed, I believe I would openly advocate disobeying these anti-religious laws. I must make two honest confessions to you, my Christian and Jewish brothers. First, I must confess that over the last few years I have been gravely disappointed with the white moderate. I have almost reached the regrettable conclusion that the Negro's great stumbling block in the stride toward freedom is not the White Citizen's Counciler or the Ku Klux Klanner, but the white moderate who is more devoted to "order" than to justice; who prefers a negative peace which is the absence of tension to a positive peace which is the presence of justice; who constantly says, "I agree with you in the goal you seek, but I can't agree with your methods of direct action"; who paternalistically feels that he can set the timetable for another man's freedom; who lives by the myth of time and who constantly advised the Negro to wait until a "more convenient season." Shallow understanding from people of good will is more frustrating than absolute misunderstanding from people of ill will. Lukewarm acceptance is much more bewildering than outright rejection.

I had hoped that the white moderate would understand that law and order exist for the purpose of establishing justice, and that when they fail to do this they become dangerously structured dams that block the flow of social progress. I had hoped that the white moderate would understand that the present tension of the South is merely a necessary phase of the transition from an obnoxious negative peace, where the Negro passively accepted his unjust plight, to a substance-filled positive peace, where all men will respect the dignity and worth of human personality. Actually, we who engage in nonviolent direct action are not the creators of tension. We merely bring to the surface the hidden tension that is already alive. We bring it out in the open where it can be seen and dealt with. Like a boil that can never be cured as long as it is covered up but must be opened with all its pus-flowing ugliness to the natural medicines of air and light, injustice must likewise be exposed, with all of the tension its exposing creates, to the light of human conscience and the air of national opinion before it can be cured.

In your statement you asserted that our actions, even though peaceful, must be condemned because they precipitate violence. But can this assertion be logically made? Isn't this like condemning the robbed man because his possession of money precipitated the evil act of robbery? Isn't this like condemning Socrates because his unswerving commitment to truth and his philosophical delvings precipitated the misguided popular mind to make him drink the hemlock? Isn't this like condemning Jesus because His unique God-consciousness and never-ceasing devotion to his will precipitated the evil act of crucifixion? We must come to see, as federal courts have consistently affirmed, that it is immoral to urge an individual to withdraw his efforts to gain his basic constitutional rights because the quest precipitates violence. Society must protect the robbed and punish the robber.

I had also hoped that the white moderate would reject the myth of time. I received a letter this morning from a white brother in Texas which said: "All Christians know that the colored people will receive equal rights eventually, but it is possible that you are in too great of a religious hurry. It has taken Christianity almost two thousand years to accomplish what it has. The teachings of Christ take time to come to earth." All that is said here grows out of a tragic misconception of time. It is the strangely irrational notion that there is something in the very flow of time that will inevitably cure all ills. Actually time is neutral. It can be used either destructively or constructively. I am coming to feel that the people of ill will have used time much more effectively than the people of good will. We will have to repent in this generation not merely for the vitriolic words and actions of the bad people, but for the appalling silence of the good people. We must come to see that human progress never rolls in on wheels of inevitability. It comes through the tireless efforts and persistent work of men willing to be co-workers with God, and without this hard work time itself becomes an ally of the forces of social stagnation. We must use time creatively, and forever realize that the time is always ripe to do right. Now is the time to make real the promise of democracy, and transform our pending national elegy into a creative psalm of brotherhood. Now is the time to lift our national policy from the quicksand of racial injustice to the solid rock of human dignity.

You spoke of our activity in Birmingham as extreme. At first I was rather disappointed that fellow clergymen would see my nonviolent efforts as those of the extremist. I started thinking about the fact that I stand in the middle of two opposing forces in the Negro community. One is a force of complacency made up of Negroes who, as a result of long years of oppression, have been so completely drained of self-respect and a sense of "somebodiness" that they have adjusted to segregation, and, of a few Negroes in the middle class who, because of a degree of academic and economic security, and because at points they profit by segregation, have unconsciously become insensitive to the problems of the masses. The other force is one of bitterness and hatred, and comes perilously close to advocating violence. It is expressed in the various black nationalist groups that are springing up over the nation, the largest and best known being Elijah Muhammad's Muslim movement. This movement is nourished by the contemporary frustration over the continued existence of racial discrimination. It is made up of people who have lost faith in America, who have absolutely repudiated Christianity, and who have concluded that the white man is an incurable "devil." I have tried to stand between these two forces, saying that we need not follow the "do-nothingism" of the complacent or the hatred and despair of the black nationalist. There is the more excellent way of love and nonviolent protest. I'm grateful to God that, through the Negro church, the dimension of nonviolence entered our struggle. If this philosophy had not emerged, I am convinced that by now many streets of the South would be flowing with floods of blood. And I am further convinced that if our white brothers dismiss us as "rabble-rousers" and "outside agitators" those of us who are working through the channels of nonviolent direct action and refuse to support our nonviolent efforts, millions of Negroes, out of frustration and despair, will seek solace and security in black nationalist ideologies, a development that will lead inevitably to a frightening racial nightmare.

Oppressed people cannot remain oppressed forever. The urge for freedom will eventually come. This is what happened to the American Negro. Something within has reminded him of his birthright of freedom; something without has reminded him that he can gain it. Consciously and unconsciously, he has been swept in by what the Germans call the *Zeitgeist*, and with his black brothers of Africa, and his brown and yellow brothers of Asia, South America and the Caribbean, he is moving with a sense of cosmic urgency toward the promised land of racial justice. Recognizing this vital urge that has engulfed the Negro community, one should readily understand public demonstrations. The Negro has many pent-up resentments and latent frustrations. He has to get them out. So let him march sometime; let him have his prayer pilgrimages to the city hall; understand why he must have sit-ins and freedom rides. If his repressed emotions do not come out in these nonviolent ways, they will come out in ominous expressions of violence. This is not a threat; it is a fact of history. So I have not said to my people "get rid of your discontent." But I have tried to say that this normal and healthy discontent can be channelized through the creative outlet of nonviolent direct action. Now this approach is being dismissed as extremist. I must admit that I was initially disappointed in being so categorized.

But as I continued to think about the matter I gradually gained a bit of satisfaction from being considered an extremist. Was not Jesus an extremist in love—"Love your enemies, bless them that curse you, pray for them that despitefully use you." Was not Amos an extremist for justice—"Let justice roll down like waters and righteousness like a mighty stream." Was not Paul an extremist for the gospel of Jesus Christ—"I bear in my body the marks of the Lord Jesus." Was not Martin Luther an extremist—"Here I stand; I can do none other so help me God." Was not John Bunyan an extremist—"I will stay in jail to the end of my days before I make a butchery of my conscience." Was not Abraham Lincoln an extremist—"This nation cannot survive half slave and half free." Was not Thomas Jefferson an extremist—"We hold these truths to be self-evident, that all men are created equal." So the question is not whether we will be extremist but what kind of extremist will we be. Will we be extremists for hate or will we be extremists for love? Will we be extremists for the preservation of injustice—or will we be extremists for the cause of justice? In that dramatic scene on Calvary's hill, three men were crucified. We must not forget that all three were crucified for the same crime—the crime of extremism. Two were extremists for immorality, and thusly fell below their environment. The other, Jesus Christ, was an extremist for love, truth and goodness, and thereby rose above his environment. So, after all, maybe the South, the nation and the world are in dire need of creative extremists.

I had hoped that the white moderate would see this. Maybe I was too optimistic. Maybe I expected too much. I guess I should have realized that few members of a race that has oppressed another race can understand or appreciate the deep groans and passionate yearnings of those that have been oppressed and still fewer have the vision to see that injustice must be rooted out by strong, persistent and determined action. I am thankful, however, that some of our white brothers have grasped the meaning of this social revolution and committed themselves to it. They are still all too small in quantity, but they are big in quality. Some like Ralph McGill, Lillian Smith, Harry Golden and James Dabbs have written about our struggle in eloquent, prophetic and understanding terms. Others have marched with us down nameless streets of the South. They have languished in filthy roach-infested jails, suffering the abuse and brutality of angry policemen who see them as "dirty nigger-lovers." They, unlike so many of their moderate brothers and sisters, have recognized the urgency of the moment and sensed the need for powerful "action" antidotes to combat the disease of segregation.

Let me rush on to mention my other disappointment. I have been so greatly disappointed with the white church and its leadership. Of course, there are some notable exceptions. I am not unmindful of the fact that each of you has taken some significant stands on this issue. I commend you, Rev. Stallings, for your Christian stance on this past Sunday, in welcoming Negroes to your worship service on a non-segregated basis. I commend the Catholic leaders of this state for integrating Springhill College several years ago.

But despite these notable exceptions I must honestly reiterate that I have been disappointed with the church. I do not say that as one of the negative critics who can always find something wrong with the church. I say it as a minister of the gospel, who loves the church; who was nurtured in its bosom; who has been sustained by its spiritual blessings and who will remain true to it as long as the cord of life shall lengthen.

I had the strange feeling when I was suddenly catapulted into the leadership of the bus protest in Montgomery several years ago that we would have the support of the white church. I felt that the white ministers, priests and rabbis of the South would be some of our strongest allies. Instead, some have been outright opponents, refusing to understand the freedom movement and misrepresenting its leaders; all too many others have been more cautious than courageous and have remained silent behind the anesthetizing security of the stained glass windows.

In spite of my shattered dreams of the past, I came to Birmingham with the hope that the white religious leadership of this community would see the justice of our cause, and with deep moral concern, serve as the channel through which our just grievances would get to the power structure. I had hoped that each of you would understand. But again I have been disappointed. I have heard numerous religious leaders of the South call upon their worshippers to comply with a desegregation decision because it is the *law*, but I have longed to hear white ministers say, "Follow this decree because integration is morally *right* and the Negro is your brother." In the midst of blatant injustices inflicted upon the Negro, I have watched white churches stand on the sideline and merely mouth pious irrelevancies and sanctimonious trivialities. In the midst of a mighty struggle to rid our nation of racial and economic injustice, I have heard so many ministers say, "Those are social issues with which the gospel has no real concern," and I have watched so many churches commit themselves to a completely otherworldly religion which made a strange distinction between body and soul, the sacred and the secular.

So here we are moving toward the exit of the twentieth century with a religious community largely adjusted to the status quo, standing as a taillight behind other community agencies rather than a headlight leading men to higher levels of justice.

I have traveled the length and breadth of Alabama, Mississippi and all the other southern states. On sweltering summer days and crisp autumn mornings I have looked at her beautiful churches with their lofty spires pointing heavenward. I have beheld the impressive outlay of her massive religious education buildings. Over and over again I have found myself asking: "What kind of people worship here? Who is their God? Where were their voices when the lips of Governor Barnett dripped with words of interposition and nullification? Where were they when Governor Wallace gave the clarion call for defiance and hatred? Where were their voices of support when tired, bruised and weary Negro men and women decided to rise from the dark dungeons of complacency to the bright hills of creative protest?"

Yes, these questions are still in my mind. In deep disappointment, I have wept over the laxity of the church. But be assured that my tears have been tears of love. There can be no deep disappointment where there is not deep love. Yes, I love the church; I love her sacred walls. How could I do otherwise? I am in the rather unique position of being the son, the grandson and the great-grandson of preachers. Yes, I see the church as the body of Christ. But, oh! How we have blemished and scarred that body through social neglect and fear of being nonconformists.

There was a time when the church was very powerful. It was during that period when the early Christians rejoiced when they were deemed worthy to suffer for what they believed. In those days the church was not merely a thermometer that recorded the ideas and principles of popular opinion; it was a thermostat that transformed the mores of society. Wherever the early Christians entered a town the power structure got disturbed and immediately sought to convict them for being "disturbers of the peace" and "outside agitators." But they went on with the conviction that they were "a colony of heaven," and had to obey God rather than man. They were small in number but big in commitment. They were too

God-intoxicated to be "astronomically intimidated." They brought an end to such ancient evils as infanticide and gladiatorial contest.

Things are different now. The contemporary church is often a weak, ineffectual voice with an uncertain sound. It is so often the arch-supporter of the status quo. Far from being disturbed by the presence of the church, the power structure of the average community is consoled by the church's silent and often vocal sanction of things as they are.

But the judgement of God is upon the church as never before. If the church of today does not recapture the sacrificial spirit of the early church, it will lose its authentic ring, forfeit the loyalty of millions, and be dismissed as an irrelevant social club with no meaning for the twentieth century. I am meeting young people every day whose disappointment with the church has risen to outright disgust.

Maybe again, I have been too optimistic. Is organized religion too inextricably bound to the status quo to save our nation and the world? Maybe I must turn my faith to the inner spiritual church, the church within the church, as the true *ecclesia* and the hope of the world. But again I am thankful to God that some noble souls from the ranks of organized religion have broken loose from the paralyzing chains of conformity and joined us as active partners in the struggle for freedom. They have left their secure congregations and walked the streets of Albany, Georgia, with us. They have gone through the highways of the South on tortuous rides for freedom. Yes, they have gone to jail with us. Some have been kicked out of their churches, and lost support of their bishops and fellow ministers. But they have gone with the faith that right defeated is stronger than evil triumphant. These men have been the leaven in the lump of the race. Their witness has been the spiritual salt that has preserved the true meaning of the gospel in these troubled times. They have carved a tunnel of hope through the dark mountain of disappointment.

I hope the church as a whole will meet the challenge of this decisive hour. But even if the church does not come to the aid of justice, I have no despair about the future. I have no fear about the outcome of our struggle in Birmingham, even if our motives are presently misunderstood. We will reach the goal of freedom in Birmingham and all over the nation, because the goal of America is freedom. Abused and scorned though we may be, our destiny is tied up with the destiny of America. Before the pilgrims landed at Plymouth we were here. Before the pen of Jefferson etched across the pages of history the majestic words of the Declaration of Independence, we were here. For more than two centuries our foreparents labored in this country without wages; they made cotton king; and they built the homes of their masters in the midst of brutal injustice and shameful humiliation—and yet out of a bottomless vitality they continued to thrive and develop. If the inexpressible cruelties of slavery could not stop us, the opposition we now face will surely fail.

We will win our freedom because the sacred heritage of our nation and the eternal will of God are embodied in our echoing demands.

I must close now. But before closing I am impelled to mention one other point in your statement that troubled me profoundly. You warmly commended the Birmingham police force for keeping "order" and "preventing violence." I don't believe you would have so warmly commended the police force if you had seen its angry violent dogs literally biting six unarmed, nonviolent Negroes. I don't believe you would so quickly commend the policemen if you would observe their ugly and inhuman treatment of Negroes here in the city jail; if you would watch them push and curse old Negro women and young Negro girls; if you would see them slap and kick old Negro men and young boys; if you will observe them, as they did on two occasions, refuse to give us food because we wanted to sing our grace together. I'm sorry that I can't join you in your praise for the police department.

It is true that they have been rather disciplined in their public handling of the demonstrators. In this sense they have been rather publicly "nonviolent." But for what purpose? To preserve the evil system of segregation. Over the last few years I have consistently preached that nonviolence demands that the means we use must be as pure as the ends we seek. So I have tried to make it clear that it is wrong to use immoral means to attain moral ends. But now I must affirm that it is just as wrong, or even more so, to use moral means to preserve immoral ends. Maybe Mr. Connor and his policemen have been rather publicly nonviolent, as Chief Pritchett was in Albany, Georgia, but they have used the moral means of nonviolence to maintain the immoral end of flagrant racial injustice. T. S. Eliot has said that there is no greater treason than to do the right deed for the wrong reason.

I wish you had commended the Negro sit-inners and demonstrators of Birmingham for their sublime courage, their willingness to suffer and their amazing discipline in the midst of the most inhuman provocation. One day the South will recognize its real heroes. They will be the James Merediths, courageously and with a majestic sense of purpose facing jeering and hostile mobs and the agonizing loneliness that characterizes the life of the pioneer. They will be old, oppressed, battered Negro women, symbolized in a seventy-two-year-old woman of Montgomery, Alabama, who rose up with a sense of dignity and with her people decided not to ride the segregated buses, and responded to one who inquired about her tiredness with ungrammatical profundity: "My feet is tired, but my soul is rested." They will be the young high school and college students, young ministers of the gospel and a host of their elders courageously and nonviolently sitting-in at lunch counters and willingly going to jail for conscience's sake. One day the South will know that when these disinherited children of God sat down at lunch counters they were in reality standing up for the best in the American dream and the most sacred values in our Judeo-Christian heritage, and thusly, carrying our whole nation back to those great wells of democracy which were dug deep by the Founding Fathers in the formulation of the Constitution and the Declaration of Independence.

Never before have I written a letter this long (or should I say book?). I'm afraid that it is much too long to take your precious time. I can assure you that it would have been much shorter if I had been writing from a comfortable desk, but what else is there to do when you are alone for days in the dull monotony of a narrow jail cell other than write long letters, think strange thoughts, and pray long prayers?

If I have said anything in this letter that is an overstatement of the truth and is indicative of an unreasonable impatience, I beg you to forgive me. If I have said anything in this letter that is an understatement of the truth and is indicative of my having a patience that makes me patient with anything less than brotherhood, I beg God to forgive me.

I hope this letter finds you strong in the faith. I also hope that circumstances will soon make it possible for me to meet each of you, not as an integrationist or a civil rights leader, but as a fellow clergyman and a Christian brother. Let us all hope that the dark clouds of racial prejudice will soon pass away and the deep fog of misunderstanding will be lifted from our fear-drenched communities and in some not too distant tomorrow the radiant stars of love and brotherhood will shine over our great nation with all of their scintillating beauty.

Yours for the cause of Peace and Brotherhood,

Martin Luther King, Jr.

Martin Luther King, Jr., Why We Can't Wait (New York: Harper & Row, 1963, 1964). The American Friends Committee first published this essay as a pamphlet. It has probably been reprinted more than anything else Dr. King wrote.